EXQUISITE

The World of Japanese Kumihimo Braiding

EXQUISITE

The World of Japanese Kumihimo Braiding

Editor **Kei Sahashi**

with photographs by **Akihiko Tokue**

KODANSHA INTERNATIONAL
Tokyo and New York

ADDITIONAL PHOTO CREDITS:

Tokyo National Museum, Nos. 2, 4 and color page 65 (left); Shoso-in, No. 3; Shitenno-ji, color page 66 (top); Hisashi Oomichi (by Tsunehiro Kobayashi), color page 66 (bottom); Kumano Hayatama Taisha (by Tsunehiro Kobayashi), color page 67 (left); Kushibiki Hachiman-gu, color page 67 (right); Kodansha Photo Library, Nos. 15–17; Iwao Nukada, No. 32.

This book was published with the assistance of the Mie-ken Kumihimo Kyodokumiai, with offices at 1929–10, Shijuku-cho, Ueno-shi, Mie Prefecture, phone: 0595–23–8038.

Distributed in the United States by Kodansha International/USA Ltd., through Harper & Row, Publishers, Inc., 10 East 53rd Street, New York, New York 10022. Published by Kodansha International Ltd., 2-2, Otowa 1-chome, Bunkyo-ku, Tokyo 112 and Kodansha International/USA Ltd., 10 East 53rd Street, New York, New York 10022.

CONTENTS

Cords that Bind the Heart

by Makoto Ooka

Various explanations have been posited for the origin of the word *himo*—"cord." None so far has been verified as indisputable, but the one that I find most appealing was suggested by the linguist and anthropologist, Prof. Shizuo Matsuoka. According to him *himo* stands for "*himeo*," or "secret cord." In the *Journal of Ancient Japanese Customs* (*Nihonkozokushi*) he writes, "Mysterious and integral to the intimacy of husband and wife, under no circumstances could a cord be touched or tied by the hands of outsiders." Indeed, in the *Man'yoshu*, the first anthology of Japanese poems, which collects songs primarily from the mid-seventh to mid-eighth century, one finds many a love poem verifying Matsuoka's explanation of the meaning of *himo* as something with a mysterious spirit.

Whether or not the explanation that "*himo*" is a contraction of "*himeo*" is true, without a doubt, cords were seen by the Japanese to have deep spiritual meaning. To tie or bind (*musubu*)—to wrap up for preservation things of importance, which, in essence, ought to be secret—is the function of cords and also expresses their symbolic import. Cords, however, not only bind objects, but also embody the knotting of two hearts. Lovers in ancient times, having tied their love vows, would, when faced with separation, tie together the cords of each other's garments and swear they would not undo them until the next meeting. When the tie was again undone, both heart and body were offered up to the partner, the unknotting symbolizing a release of the unconditional love.

Because tying a cord carried the meaning of being entrusted with the life of the "tied" person, it served as an acknowledgement of one's love and also as a prayer for the safety and health of that person. One is reminded of clasped hands in an attitude of prayer or devotion to God or Buddha, an attitude that seems to cross racial and cultural borders.

It is no surprise that the age of the flowering of the Heian period nobility (eleventh century), when astrology and magic still ruled people's lives, was the time when the real artistry of cords developed. Cords told fortunes and also served to distinguish between male and female by the thickness or thinness of the cords' tassels, by the number and kinds of colors used, and by an unimaginable wealth of styles of tying. Here the practical and the decorative were tightly bound in mutual benefit. The cords that decorated the garments and daily objects of the palace ladies as well as the cords that laced together the many elements of the armor worn by samurai in the middle ages shared a practical, decorative, and magical-symbolic essence. This essence has been preserved and continues to live in Japanese decorative cords today.

Once I was most astonished to hear an abbess in a temple in Kyoto relate that the Japanese had some one thousand methods of decorative tying for cords. After that, to my further amazement, she added, "At this point I am ashamed to admit that I can only make about a hundred of them." Later I learned that this nun, Nishigaki Rinkoni, was an extremely accomplished scholar researching the restoration of ancient decorative cord tying and an artist engaged in recreating the tradition through practical experimentation. Evidently, even today cords possess the power to tie the hearts of men and women.

Translated by Monica Bethe

Hidejo Kanzaki

Junko Koshino

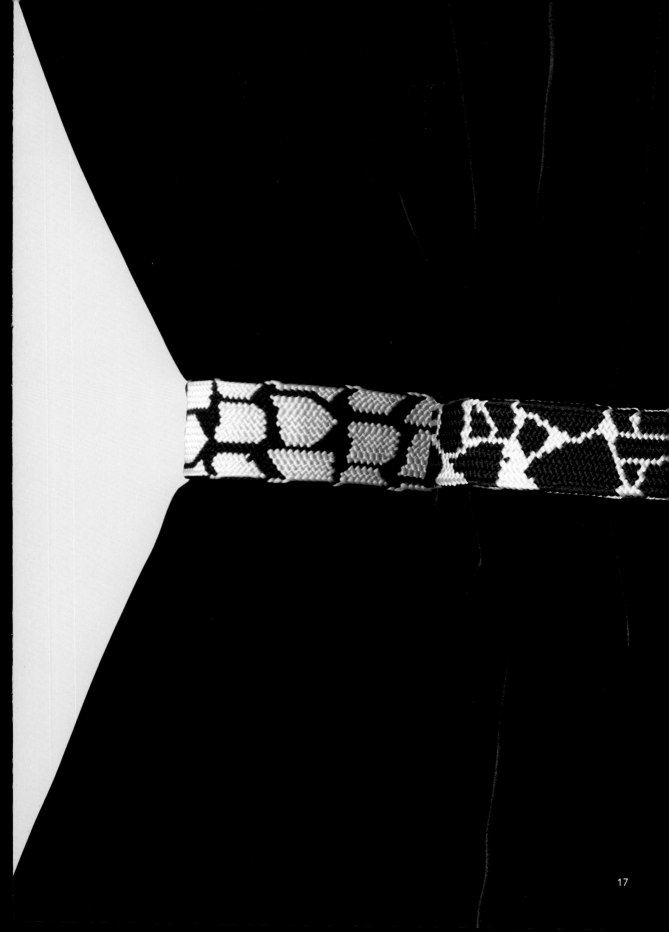

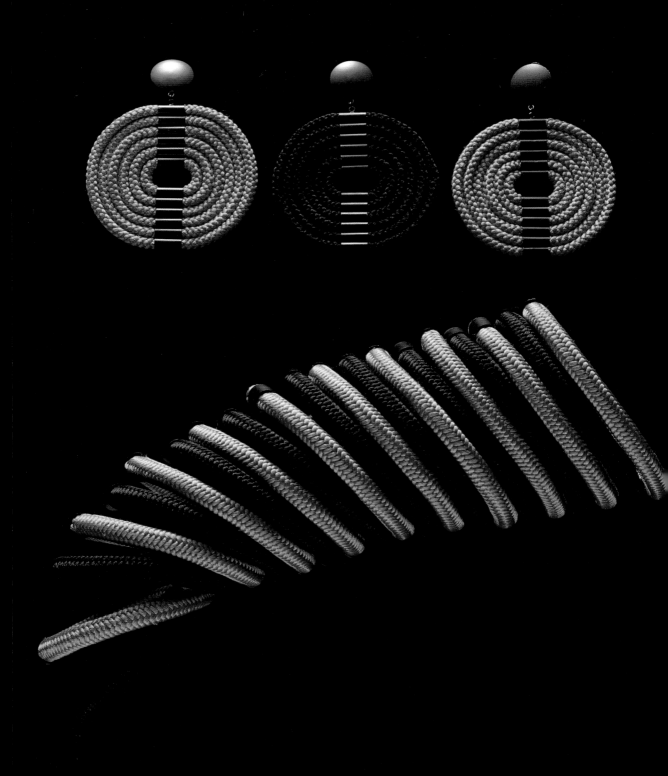

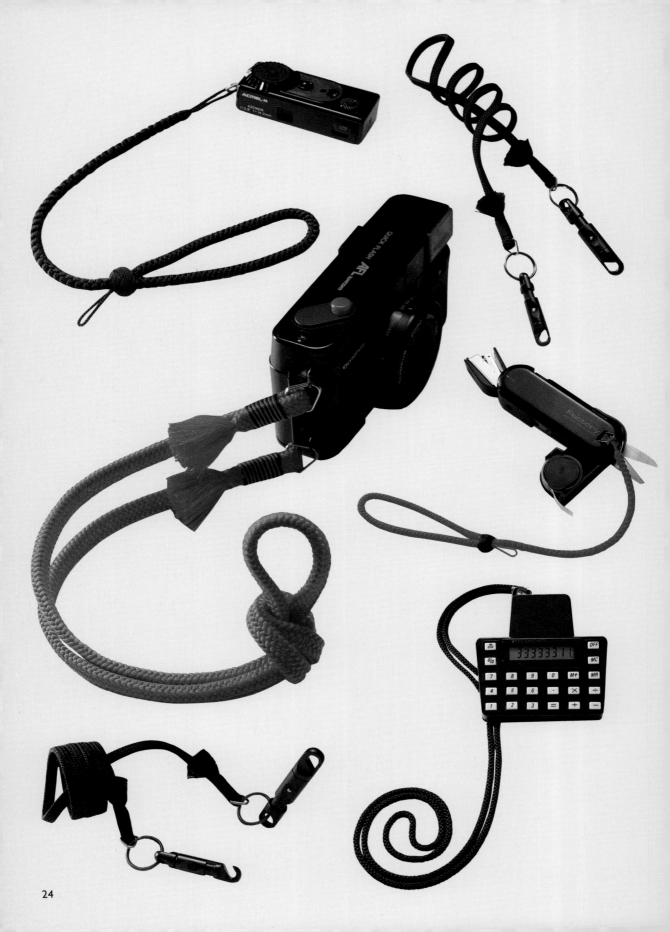

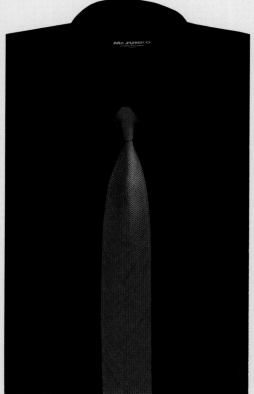

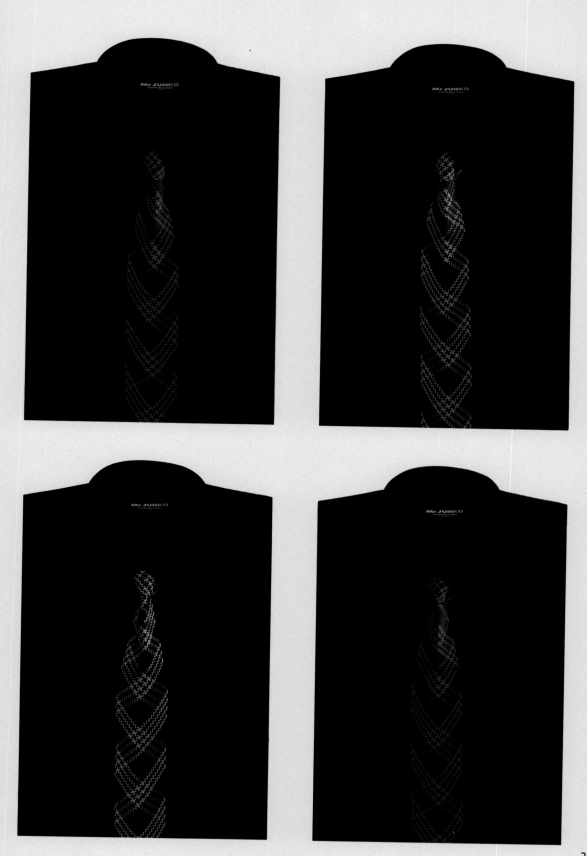

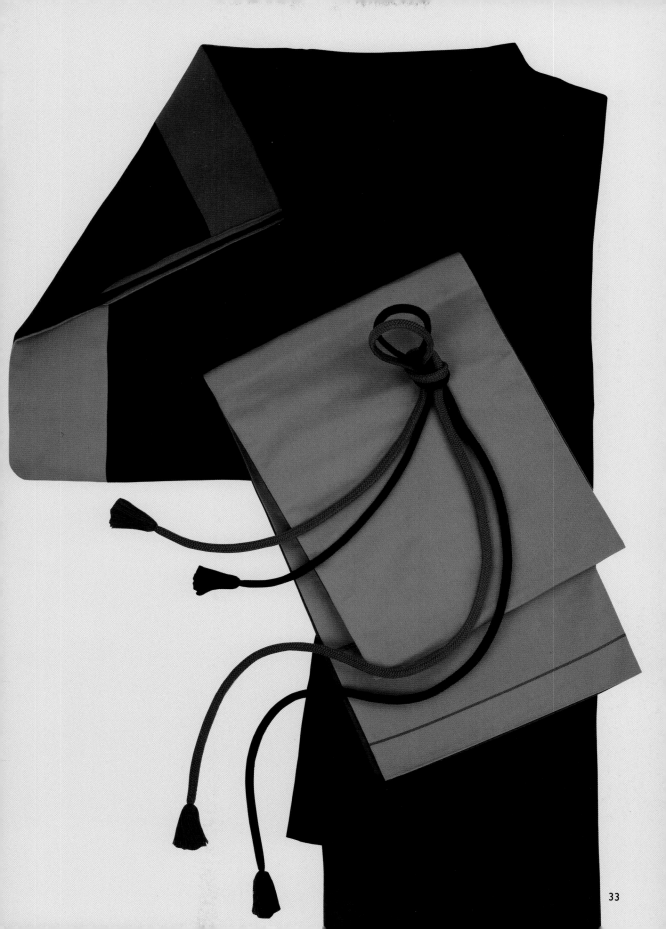

Minami Tada

KUMIHIMO —An Overview

by Catherine Martin

From earliest times, people throughout the world have always needed simple ropes and cords to hold, tie and fasten all manner of objects. In certain cultures hand-made ropes have remained in a primitive form, in others the skills of making them have transcended the purely functional aspects of the craft and become a highly sophisticated art form. Nowhere can this be seen more clearly than in Japan, where the art of interlacing threads was developed and extended to produce an astonishing variety of highly complex, elegant and refined silk braids, all remarkably designed to combine function and beauty. This art, kumihimo, is still little known outside of Japan, and yet with the constant visual exposure to traditional and contemporary Japanese lifestyles that we have in the West, it is surprising that no attention has been drawn to these wonderful touches of color, pattern and texture that so vividly reflect the Japanese delight in technique and materials.

The sight of samurai armour has become familiar to many, but few even notice the metres of exquisitely dyed and braided hand-made cord that hold the armour together. Museums offer little or no information about the braids, and even in Japan there is much practical and historical research to be completed, with many braids still waiting to be analysed and reconstructed.

Braid-making in Japan is categorised into different ways of crossing threads. Amongst them are: twisted (*yorihimo*), knitted (*amihimo*), woven (*orihimo*) and whipped (*kukehimo*) braids, but only experts are familiar with them, and *kumihimo* is the name in general use for Japanese braiding. It is a difficult word to translate satisfactorily, being a compound of two Chinese characters: *kumi* meaning "coming together" or "group," and *himo*, which by itself describes string, cord, rope, or braid. Together these elements form an independent noun, which strictly refers to one particular way of making braids, that of "oblique interlacing". On a practical level, kumihimo is a straightforward, logical process. Follow the instructions implicitly and a braid will be made. Aesthetically, it is a ritual, a way, a discipline whereby seemingly simple movements are repeated to produce an interplay of colour, texture and pattern in a length of silk braid.

The principles of the craft also reveal a deceptive simplicity and economy of design. All the looms, known as stands (*dai*), are made from wood and/or bamboo and can be taken apart for storage and reassembled when needed. All traditional braid-makers work on tatami mats, which provide a smooth sympathetic surface, and a kumihimo studio is usually a quite small, uncluttered area, where the only sounds are those of the weighted bobbins clacking against the wood of the stand.

Throughout the twelve hundred years of kumihimo history in Japan, many looms have been designed to make different braids, but there are four that are in constant use today. They are the *marudai*, *kakudai*, *ayatakedai* and *takadai* (Pls. 6, 8, 10, 12). All are set up with carefully measured silk threads, which have been divided into groups of usually equal numbers of strands, each group being attached to bobbins of identical weight made from turned wood with a lead core. These can weigh from 37 grams (somewhat more than an ounce) up to 150 grams (about one-third pound) or more; the choice of bobbins being directly related to the number of fine strands of silk in each group. The bobbins are lifted and moved in certain repeated patterns and sequences to produce each type of braid.

The method of braiding defines the shape of the braid and consists of a series of movements, the sequence of braiding. Limitless patterns are available by using the same method but changing the arrangement of the colours before making the first movement of the sequence— much as one shakes a kaleidoscope before turning it. Other variables depend on the number of colours, proportion of colours, and number of bobbins that are used.

The *marudai*, the most popular and versatile of the braiding stands, consists of a smooth round top with a central aperture supported by four pillars on a sturdy base. It is traditionally worked from a kneeling position, and the braid grows through the center of the *marudai* pulled down (or up) by a counterweight attached to the braid, either below or from above. The tension can be altered by adjustments to the counterweight. The hanging bobbins are arranged in groups around the top of the stand, and their spatial relationship must always be maintained. On a *marudai*, pairs of bobbins are lifted and repositioned, taking from one group and adding to another in the prescribed sequence. The simplest braid in terms of construction is the *yotsugumi*, which only uses four bobbins. However, any number of bobbins can be used on a *marudai*, in multiples of four and eight, with a correspondingly larger top. Flat, round and square braids can be made on this stand.

When working on a *kakudai* (also from a kneeling position), the braid grows upward from the square-topped stand and is counterweighted from above. The bobbins are also moved in pairs, but only around the four sides, not across the stand. The limitations of the positioning and movement of the bobbins are countered by some really exciting technical and design possibilities.

The *ayatakedai* (bamboo stand) produces flat, strong, thick braids by a process related to twining rather than to oblique interlacing, although the braids are still included under the heading of kumihimo. The bobbins are hung from six separated pieces of notched and carved bamboo attached to a wooden frame facing the (kneeling) braid-maker. Each row of stitches is made by moving pairs of bobbins from the lower level to the upper notches with a sharp jerking movement, automatically displacing the upper bobbins, which fall to the lower level. After beating the new row with a long, flat piece of bamboo, two side or weft theads are passed and crossed inside the braid and repositioned, and again it is beaten horizontally into place. The most interesting effects of working on an *ayatakedai* are achieved by using one colour and changing the original position of certain bobbins, or leaving pairs out of the weaving for one or two rows, thereby creating surface textural effects.

Taka means "high", and, as its name suggests, the *takadai* is a large loom on which the braid-maker can either sit on a stool or kneel on a raised platform in the traditional manner. On each side of the loom are two rows (upper and lower) of moveable wooden blocks with pegs set into each to separate the bobbins. Braids can be made by using just the lower levels or all four, but in each case the method of working is the same. A passage or shed is created by hand, moving upwards and downwards, including some groups of silk and omitting others, depending on the braid, and keeping the passage open by use of the bamboo spatula. A bobbin is swung through the passage from one side to the other, the spatula released, and the braid is beaten into place at an angle following the line the bobbin has made. Only flat braids can be made on a *takadai*, which in its present form was devised in the Edo period (1603–1867) in order to make an entirely new type of "double-cloth" braid. These usually featured a motif that could be repeated at will rather than inevitably, and these strong, stiff braids were known as *ayadashi* cords, using all four of the levels on a *takadai*.

Although cotton and hemp yarns have been used in the past for specific purposes, such as hemp cores for thick round silk braids and cotton for cords, the majority of braids have always been made in silk. Unspun or thicker hand-twisted silk was used in the seventh and eighth centuries, the former producing soft, flexible braids, but with less clearly defined patterns compared to those using the twisted silk. Nowadays a fine, reeled, three-ply highly twisted silk yarn is used for hand-braiding, available in twenty-five gram (five-sixths of an ounce) skeins for dyeing, or more usually as pre-dyed, prepared and warped lengths ready to put straight on the braiding stand. The latter is favoured by the schools, most of whom do not teach warping.

Up until the mid-nineteenth century, by which time all the really beautiful braids had been designed, the dyes used were from natural sources. The skill of the professional dyers was greatly respected, and when looking at the ancient but well-preserved braids, a sense of immense care and understanding of the use of natural dyes seems to communicate itself directly through the subtle but vibrant colours. Most kumihimo silk is now dyed with chemical dyes, but there has recently been a resurgence of interest in traditional methods and a return to the painstaking but rewarding process of collecting and preparing plant dye material. Indigo was used frequently to dye silk for braids, producing a range of blues from the lovely pale green-turquoise after five dippings through to the dark, dark blue after thirty or more dips in different vats.

The choice of colours to use in a braid is always difficult, and a wide range of colour is needed in order to make this choice. The reaction of certain colours to one another in braids is always unpredictable, and it is only after some time that a sense of what will work well in a braid is felt. But, then kumihimo is not an easy art to master. It is only after endless hours of practice that a technically perfect braid can ever be achieved, and only then is it possible for the truth and spirit of the individual braid-maker to shine through. This is where the mystery enters and goes beyond mere technical mastery. A feel for braiding cannot be taught, nor can the internal qualities that are revealed so clearly in a really beautiful length of silk braid.

Historical Aspects

The remarkable skill and ingenuity of the Japanese people in tying, knotting, wrapping, and packaging is well known and admired. It seems to be an instinctive part of the culture, and cords or braids are indispensable to the art. The earliest indication of using braids for decoration can be seen from looking at ceramics from the Neolithic Jomon period (10,000–ca. 300 B.C.). Twined, twisted and braided vegetable fibres were pressed into the wet clay of pots. A more economical way of impressing a design was to use fibres wound and knotted around a slender bamboo stick, which was then rolled onto the soft clay, producing complex patterns. These pots are found all over Japan, and the name of this particular period of Japanese history—Jomon—actually means "cord marked", referring to the ceramics.

Earthenware figures known as *haniwa* found in burial mounds from the fourth to the sixth centuries give further clues as to how early braids were used (Pl. 1). Some of these figures are obviously warriors, and various ties and braids can be seen on cuffs, protective headgear and around the prototype of armour, tying the swords or daggers to the waist. It is not possible to know if these were early woven braids or, more likely, leather or cloth ties, as it was not until the sixth to seventh centuries that formal silk braiding techniques were introduced to Japan from China and Korea. After having experimented with braiding, it must have been particularly exciting for the Japanese to absorb and realise the potential of the art. No records of the actual techniques that were passed on have survived, if indeed any records were made. Traditionally the methods of making braids were passed down from master to pupil, and the secrets of the workshop were guarded jealously. It is only from the long process of analysis and

1. Haniwa depicting a man in ceremonial dress. Aikawa Archaeological Museum, Gumma Prefecture. Important Cultural Property. H. 124.2 cm (49⅓ in.). Sixth century (Tumulus period).
Cords decorate the figure of this aristocrat in various places. Those used to fasten the two braids of hair that hang about his shoulders are called *mizura*. Another cord bound around his waist holds his jacket closed. The nicely tied cords about the knees of his trousers facilitate horseback riding.

reconstruction from fragments of surviving braids, particularly those from the well-known Shoso-in collection of the Nara period (701–794) that braiding stands or looms have been designed in order to provide a framework where certain threads can cross at certain times in order to enable exact copies to be made. It is clear from the surviving braids that more than one type of stand was in use in the eighth century, because of the different shapes and textures. The *marudai* seems to have been used for many of the early braids, and certainly it was used for *ban no fuchi kazari himo* (Pl. 2) — a stunning flat (3.7 centimeters/1½ inches wide) piece of work featuring long chevrons in contrasting colours. The heavier hand-twisted silk was chosen for this braid, and ninety-two bobbins were needed for its construction.

2. Decorative cord for the edges of a banner (*Ban no fuchi kazari himo*). Horyu-ji temple. Important Cultural Property. Flat braid, W. 3.5 cm (1⅜ in.), L. 65.0 cm (25¾ in.). Asuka period (562–701). Tokyo National Museum, Horyu-ji Treasure Hall.
Alternating chevrons of madder red and purple appear here in *sasanami* braiding. The cord functions as a decoration for the edge of a Buddhist banner. The use of colors suggests this one comes from the continent.

Many of the braids in the priceless Shoso-in collection of art and everyday objects were much smaller and used for a variety of purposes: for hanging personal adornments, pen knives, mirrors, as cords for armour lacing, and as ties for bags. Square braids were obviously very fashionable, and the predominating colours were strong shades of brown, cream, purple, and ochre with touches of orange and green.

There are a number of wide, flat sashes extremely well preserved in the collection (Pl. 3), for tying around the long loose clothing worn at that time. They were soft and supple, worked on the diagonal using many bobbins, occasionally incorporating tiny glass beads. It is interesting to note that the originals contain quite obvious mistakes in the weaving, but the sense of spontaneity and liveliness of the work is so strong that the imperfections seem of little consequence, whereas reconstructions are technically perfect but somehow lifeless in comparison.

Those who know and understand most about the earliest braids are in some disagreement about the braid called *karakumi*. Its distinctive diamond pattern is constructed in two separate stages. The first (now known as *sasanami-gumi*) provides the lower V-shape, but the second, the way of closing the diamond, uses another much more advanced technique. The first surviving example of *karakumi* was found in the Horyu-ji temple in Nara (page 65, left) and is said to have been a hanging ornament belonging to a room curtain used by the Empress

3. Braided sashes. Eighth century. Shoso-in Repository, Nara.
Among the treasures in the Shoso-in are numerous varieties of kumihimo, constituting the types from which all the various kumihimo produced in later centuries developed. The designs are geometrically constructed on the diagonal; the color combinations are extremely rich, reflecting continental taste.
—(upper) sash
Flat braid, W. 4.7 cm (1⅞ in.), L. 132.2 cm (52½ in.). The braiding of this flat sash involves bridging two strands at a time. It is thought to be a belt for ceremonial dress.
—(lower) sash
Flat braid, W. 6.0 cm (2⅜ in.), L. 214.4 cm (85 in.). The braiding for this flat sash involves interlacings of single strands, a technique that corresponds to what today is called *andagumi*.

Regnant Suiko (593–628). However, no examples of this braid are found in the Shoso-in collection, and because of the advanced techniques it is likely to belong to a later period.

Although the debate continues about the origins of the *karakumi* braid, there is no such uncertainty about its status in the hierarchy of braids. It has always been considered to be one of the most refined braids and was incorporated into imperial and court costume. The technique for producing the diamonds forms the basis of the woven flat decorative sashes known as *hirao* (page 66, bottom), with their long tassels that hang from the waist forming a central panel on men's formal court dress, providing an area of colour and texture against plain silk clothing. They are still used for formal court occasions, for certain Bugaku and Shinto ceremonial dance costumes. *Hirao* are extremely complicated to make, often featuring space dyeing and embroidery over the braiding. They were developed in the Heian period (794–1192), which really marked the transition from reproducing Chinese and Korean techniques to creating the first truly Japanese braids. During this time, artistic and social structures became less derivative, and foreign influences were less acceptable. As might be expected, the cultural changes in Japanese history affected the shape, colour and pattern in all areas of design, including braids. Those of the Heian period were delicate and elegant, using soft colours, and this mood continued during the Kamakura period, when the most complex of all the Japanese braids were made. The existing originals that have been found survived the ravages of time by being hidden in tombs and statues, in shrines and temples and were only discovered in this century when restoration and exploratory work was carried out. Each is unique, produced for a single occasion and never seen again, with no records indicating why, how or who made the braids, which must have taken many months to produce. They represent the highest flowering of Japanese braiding, and it took much time to reconstruct them in all their original glory.

Some other extant Heian period kumihimo are the cords used to bind sutra scrolls. Copying of sutras done on lavish and opulent gold decorated and dyed papers was an act of piety often sponsored by the aristocracy. The cords that tied such scrolls had to echo the expense and beauty of the entire undertaking. One such sutra cover and kumihimo is pictured on page 65 (right).

The cords on the talismans on page 66 (top) are also Heian. They

4. *Song Competition of Seventy-One Trades* (Nanajuichiban shokunin uta-awase)
Braider. This Edo period copy of a Muromachi period (1392–1573) original (probably) illustrates braiding a kumihimo on a foot pedal stand. The loop braiding is done by exchanging the loops from finger to finger. A pull of the toe activates the beater to pound tight the interlacings. Although it takes a bit of practice, once one is adept, one can braid quite complex cords very quickly using this technique.

5. Album with sample sword hilt braids. Late Edo period. The Iga merchant of sword ornaments, Tomonoya Chubei, put samples of braids used for swords into this book to show customers.

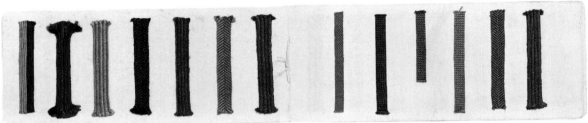

display double weave in places and are predecessors of the intricate and technically awesome double-surface tortoiseshell pattern kumihimo.

Nowhere have braids been used so extensively and ingeniously as in traditional Japanese armour (page 67, right). For centuries Japan was racked by civil war, and although the amount of braid used for the different ranks varied, the demand for the many kinds of braid used to lace and link the various components of a suit of armour must have been enormous. Many craftsmen must have been involved in dyeing and braid-making. As the years of war dragged on, the majority of braid came to be made from dark blue indigo-dyed silk, since the numerous dippings needed to produce such a dark colour actually strengthened the silk.

Swords also had their own specially designed braids: a flat ridged, laced braid around the hilt to provide sure grip in battle and a thick, strong, decorative braid to attach the sword to its samurai owner. The double-weave *takadai* braids were highly suitable for this purpose, providing the strength and also the originality associated with the change in regime at the start of the Edo period (1603–1867). The most popular motif for swords was that of the turtle, which symbolises long life in China, Korea and Japan. A simple form using only a few repeated movements, with the hexagons representing the tortoiseshell pattern appearing on one side only, can be made using the four levels of the *takadai*, but the most prized of all the tortoiseshell pattern braids is the double-surface hexagon cord, usually made in dark blue and white, with the motif appearing on both sides in reverse colours. However, the double-surface tortoiseshell braid on page 67 (left) dates from the late Heian period and antedates the appearance of the *takadai*. The technique of this kumihimo was not reconstructed until the 1970s.

In the Edo period, imperial and religious robes as well as everyday clothing even for the most lowly, all involved the use of braids to a greater or lesser degree. The earlier No theatre and kabuki and bunraku puppet drama, which developed during this time, all call for sumptuous silk costumes and braids to decorate and fasten them, often incorporating space dyeing and elaborate flower knots and tassels.

After 1868, when the samurai class was abolished and their wonderful armour and swords were often relegated to junk shops, western influences and rapid industrialisation transformed Japan. Synthetic dyes were introduced as were machines devised to replace manpower in many areas, including kumihimo. Semi-mechanised braiding stands were introduced, which were undoubtedly economically disastrous to the traditional braid-makers. Many must have given up the craft, but those left, with characterstic ingenuity, set about adapting braids for use with the wide sash or obi, which had become fashionable. So the *obijime* was born, which accounts for most of the braids, both hand-made and machine made, in Japan today. Kumihimo is a declining industry today, with fewer and fewer women wearing kimono on a daily basis, preferring the more convenient western-style dress except for special occasions.

The Way Forward

Until about 1970, very little had been published on kumihimo, and the few such books dealt with the historical and academic aspects only. This situation changed when the kumihimo workshops realised that it was becoming more and more difficult to make a living from making braids, but there was an untapped source of income from teaching kumihimo. Many private schools sprang up in the main towns of Japan—some refined, others catering for a more popular taste, but all encouraging affluent women to come and learn about an ancient tradition and to make their own *obijime*. Various courses are available on all the braiding stands, but the teaching is formal, highly structured, and an individual creative approach is not welcomed.

Each school, usually belonging to a family that has been associated with kumihimo for many generations, has produced its own teaching material, and there have been many colorful how-to-do books published on the subject. But beware. When translated none is actually comprehensive in its instructions, because these books are designed to accompany a course, with a teacher. In an attempt to make kumihimo more attractive and approachable, the art has often been taken out of its traditional context, and braids are used to make or be part of articles thought to belong to the western tradition. The results are usually unfortunate in design, concept and colour, since the gradual process of incorporating traditional techniques into the contemporary applied arts—characteristic of the western approach to embroidery, piecing and stitching, knitting, and handweaving—has been slow to mature in the world of kumihimo. However, Aya Nakayama, who lives and works in Tokyo and exhibits outside Japan, has used braids as part of her jewellery to great effect.

In the West, the transition from thinking of braids as just trimmings to be found on garments and lampshades into using them as part of professional textile art is just beginning now that a complete practical guide on *marudai* braiding has been published in English for the first time. This has enabled people from all over to experiment with the techniques in order to discover new applications. As in any craft, however carefully taught, some of these are crude and unworthy, while others are sympathetic to the Japanese approach and also very exciting. Kumihimo is taught in certain textile courses at art colleges in England, and private courses are also available. Students will inevitably produce innovative ways of using and making braids, combining them with other fibres, metals and ceramics, thereby moving kumihimo into different directions.

My own feeling is that all new work should be based on what has gone before and should reflect the infinite sensitivity and care of the early Japanese braidmakers, who devoted much time to create exactly the right effect on whatever materials they were using, so that the braids added delightfully and appropriately to their purpose, always enhancing the article concerned but having their own special appeal. Inspiration can be gained from looking at the various ways of using braids, which can be seen in Japanese collections in museums. By absorbing the qualities of ingenuity, precision and perfection and translating them into new, creative ways of working, the art of kumihimo will be continued and revitalised.

Catherine Martin is a graduate of the Domyo School of Kumihimo in Tokyo and is the foremost authority on kumihimo outside Japan. (The Domyo School is of a tradition different from that of Iga.) She is a kumihimo artist, scholar, and teacher of wide repute and resides in England. She has privately published a book on *marudai* techniques, and as of this writing is compiling a more comprehensive volume on kumihimo techniques.

Kumihimo Techniques

by Yoshio Nakauchi

Kumihimo can be classified broadly into three types: round or tubular (*maru*), square (*kaku*), and flat (*hira*). To produce these braids, four types of stands are generally used today (see Pls. 6–13). Each has its own peculiarities and produces specific types of kumihimo. The stands are: *marudai* (round stand), *kakudai* (square stand), *ayatakedai* (bamboo stand), and *takadai* (large stand).

Types of Stands:

marudai (round stand)

The round stand can be used to braid downwards (*kumisage shiki*), which produces round, square, or flat cords. The special characteristics of flat braids are, however, best effected on the *ayatakedai* or the *takadai*.

kakudai (square stand)

The square stand braids essentially the same types of cords as the *marudai*, except the number of bobbins is far more limited. Most cords made on a square stand require a twist; in the process of braiding upwards one works around the circumference of the braid, so that, in effect, the braid revolves.

ayatakedai (bamboo stand)

The bamboo stand looks and operates somewhat like a weaving loom; it employs both warp and weft threads to produce flat braids. It also is the most speedy and efficient stand of the four, in part because all the bobbins are arranged in front and are easy to manipulate. A single movement of the hand can interchange the upper and lower positions of the threads, which are hung on the four V-shaped grooves or notches carved into the upper and lower left and right sides of each bamboo slat. As a result, what would take four hand movements to do on the *marudai* can be accomplished in one move.

6. Round stand (*marudai*).

7. Examples of flat cords braided on a *marudai*.

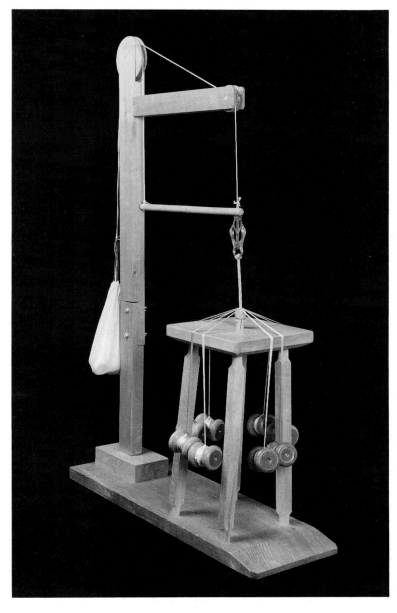

8. Square stand (*kakudai*).

9. Examples of flat cords braided on a *kakudai*.

53

10. Bamboo stand (*ayatakedai*).

11. Examples of flat cords braided on an *ayatakedai*.

takadai (large stand)

When braiding on the *takadai*, one sits on a plank inside the framework of the stand and manipulates threads hanging to the right and left of one to interlace flat braids. After preparing a path by weaving the hand through the next interlacing, the bobbin is grabbed and brought to the opposite side of the stand. To tighten the braid, one beats with a bamboo beater (*hera*). Since the stand takes over one hundred bobbins, one can make very elaborate braids with intricate interlacings, such as designs of Chinese characters or pictorial images.

12. Large stand (*takadai*).

13. Examples of flat cords braided on a *takadai*.

Example of a cord made on a marudai

As an example of braiding, we will investigate the construction of the braid known as *maruyotsu-gumi* ("round four-strand braid"), the most versatile cord made on the simplest, easiest to use stand, the *marudai*.

Tools and materials

Marudai, bobbins (4–36) with thread wrapped on them, counterweight, chopsticks, scissors, paste, comb, needle. The bobbins weigh about 100 grams (roughly $\frac{1}{4}$ pound) each. Commonly they are made with a lead core to obtain the necessary weight. The counterweight acts as a balance to create tension on the braid while braiding, so it should ideally be about half the combined weight of the bobbins. The chopstick is used when fixing the braiding threads to the *marudai*.

Silk thread

Generally in Japan enough silk thread for one *obijime* (the cord used to tie down an obi) is sold as a set amount in a bag. The threads are composed of twenty-five strands of single-ply thread twisted together to form one element. One set of these threads is known as a handful (*hitomochi*) or a bobbinful (*hitotama*), and the standard number for making one *obijime* is twenty-four. Stretched to full length, they measure 2.6 meters ($8\frac{1}{2}$ feet) and they braid a cord 1.5 meters (5 feet) in length.

Method

A four-strand braid (*yotsugumi*) is constructed with four bobbins and is technically the most basic. At a glance it appears simple, but its very simplicity makes uneven braiding and loose tension stand out. Skilled hands are necessary to create a beautiful four-strand braid.

Step 1. *Binding the end.* Take one set of kumihimo threads and, leaving an end of about 4 centimeters ($1\frac{1}{2}$ inches) for a tassel, bind it off tightly with a strong thread or fine cord so it will not loosen.

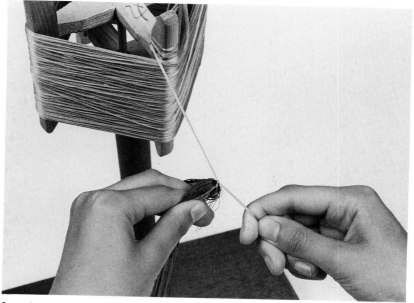

Step 1

Step 2. *Tying the knot.* There are many ways to secure the beginning end of kumihimo threads. Shown here is a double slip knot with the second loop in the process of being made. Once the braiding threads are bound, pull the loop tight.

Step 3. *Preparing the stand.* Slip the kumihimo threads through the hole in the center of the stand and then insert a chopstick in the loop made with the binding thread.

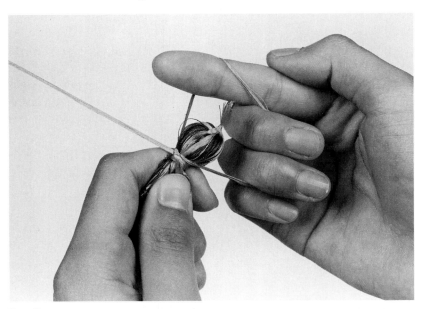

Step 2

Step 3

Step 4. *Grouping the threads.* Once the threads are on the stand, divide the twenty-four strands into four equal groups (to be wound on four bobbins) and comb the threads of each group so they lie straight without twists or knots.

Step 4

Step 5. *Winding thread on the bobbins.* Keeping the threads stretched tight, wind them onto the bobbins until the bobbins lie close to the stand. Secure them with a slip knot by taking the threads in the right hand and rotating the palm to make a loop, which can then be slipped over the bobbin and hold the threads down.

Step 6. *The counterweight.* Finally attach the counterweight to the end of the braiding threads.

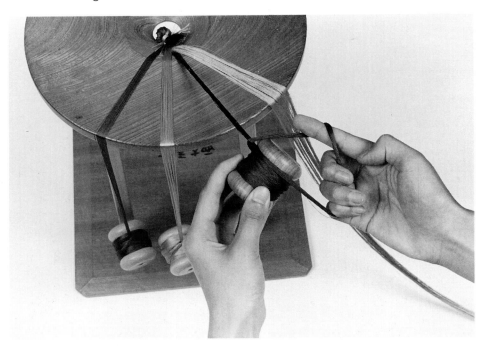

Step 5

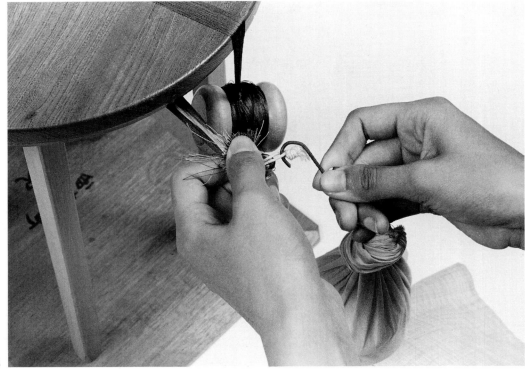

Step 6

Step 7. *Braiding.* Hold the far threads with the right hand, the near threads with the left. The illustration shows the completion of exchanging far and near threads. A well-balanced posture with a straight back, head supported directly above the neck, and relaxed shoulders allows comfortable, prolonged, and pleasant work.

Step 8. *Hand movement.* To keep the movement of the hands regular, take the right threads with the left hand (which had moved to the upper position) and exchange right and left sides. Illustrated is the moment just after the exchange begins.

Step 9. The end of the left-right interchange.

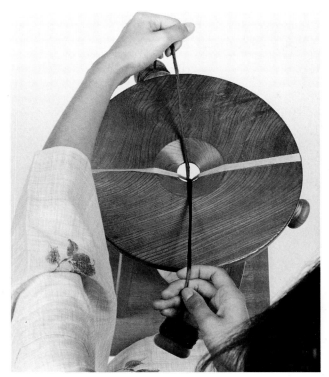
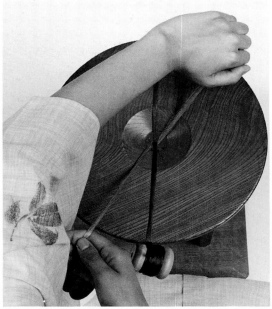

Step 8

Step 7

Step 9

Step 10. The stand with the braiding of about one-third of an *obijime* completed.

Step 11. *Preparation of the tassel.* Choose a beautiful place at the end of the braid and bind it off tightly with a thread.

Step 12. *Fixing the tassel.* To prevent the tie from sliding or undoing, secure with another thread inserted in line with the length of the cord. Illustrated here is the preparatory insertion of a needle at the base of the knot. Divide the tassel into two and bring the tying thread (on the needle) up. Then tie the two ends of this thread into a secure knot.

Translated by Monica Bethe

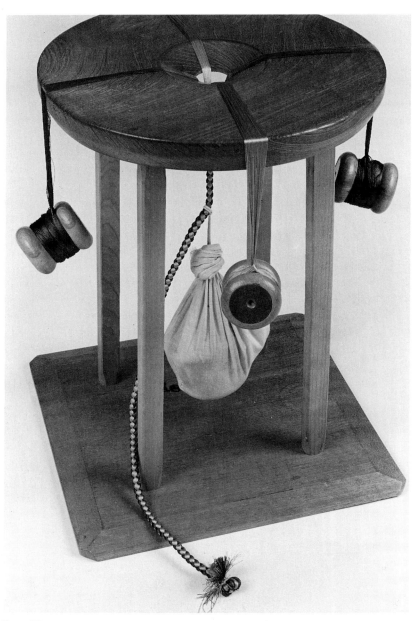

Step 10

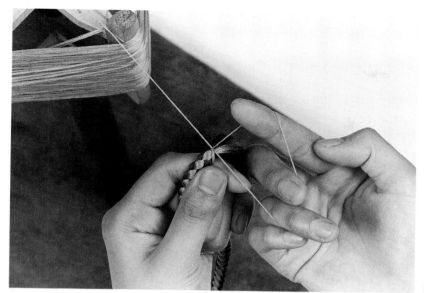

Step 11

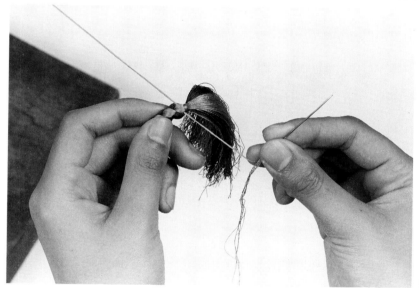

Step 12a

Step 12b

Hanging ornament. Horyu-ji.
Asuka period.

Brocade sutra cover with flat kumihimo. Formerly the property of Jingo-ji.
Late Heian period.

Cord for brocade-wrapped talisman.
Shitenno-ji. Late Heian period.

Hirao sashes. Hisashi Oomichi. Edo period.

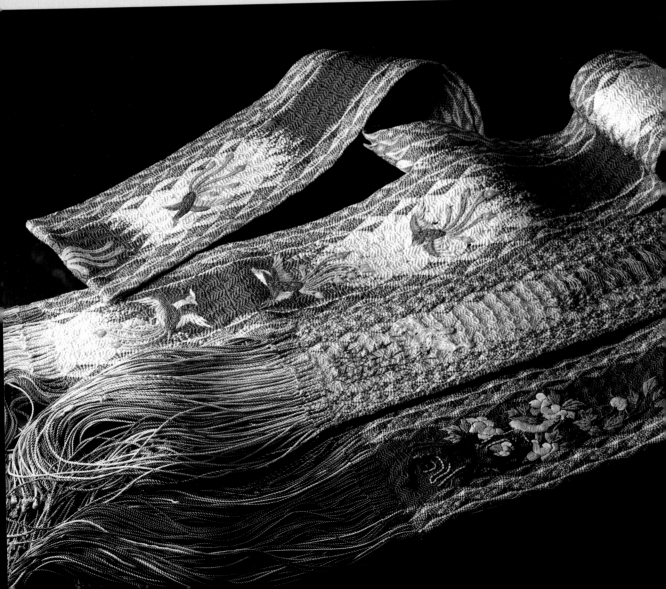

Cord with tortoiseshell pattern (hexagons) on both sides.
Kumano Hayatama Taisha. Heian period.

Red laced armor. Kushibiki Hachiman-gu.
Late Kamakura period.

Obijime made in Iga. Twentieth century.

Haori cord made in Iga.
Twentieth century.

Peruvian slings and festive cords. Twentieth century.

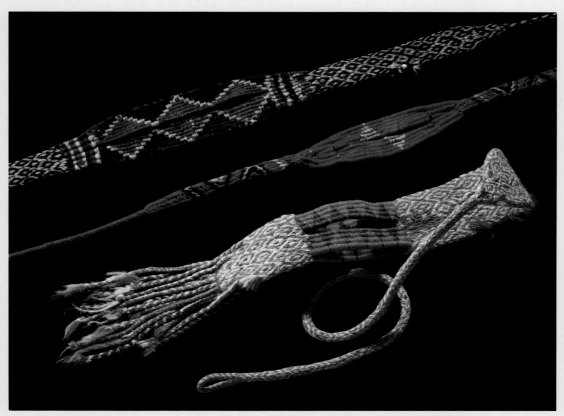

Bolivian slings. Twentieth century.

Iga and Modern Kumihimo

by Yoshio Nakauchi

Agood 80 percent of the kumihimo braids produced today come from the area of Iga in Mie Prefecture, in central Japan. This fact is somewhat remarkable considering that the making of kumihimo in the Iga area is a young industry, with a history of less than one century. The reasons lie in the historical accidents of the last one hundred years.

The event that most effectively cut the links between Edo period (1603–1867) kumihimo, used primarily for armor, swords, and equestrian accessories, and modern kumihimo was the law passed nine years after the Meiji Restoration (1868) divesting the samurai of his sword and other military appurtenances. As a result, the craftsmen and producers of armor and horse accessories were hard hit. These artisans, who had made their living from renovating small art objects, now lost their livelihood, and the techniques of making kumihimo transmitted from the Edo period died out. This applied to Iga as well. In Tokyo, however, kumihimo makers responded to the challenge with a feverish cooperation aimed at adapting the braiding techniques for sword cords and armor lacings to the production of cords for the newly fashionable overgarment, the *haori*, and for sash cords, *obijime*. These adapted techniques were then reintroduced into Iga and became the foundation for what is produced there today.

The seeds of Iga kumihimo were sewn in 1902 by the twenty-three-year-old Tokusaburo Hirosawa. At the age of fourteen, a friend had procured him an apprenticeship in a metal factory producing pots and pans, but he did not take to the trade. Instead, a meeting with Eino-suke Kobayashi, who was versed in Edo kumihimo techniques, resulted in his beginning to study the art of braiding on the *takadai*. The learning of a craft must be visceral; it must be absorbed until it becomes a part of one's being. With this in mind, Tokusaburo became a live-in disciple, applying himself with great diligence for nine years.

At the end of his technical training, he opened a factory in his hometown, Iga Ueno.

Thus present-day Iga kumihimo was born. Tokusaburo's specialty in the art of *takadai* braiding set the characteristics of what was to become Iga kumihimo: flat cords with designs of pictorial motifs and lettering (pages 68–71, Pl. 14)

Records and other sources dating from the early Meiji period (1868–1912) suggest that the order of popularization of kumihimo was: first, for men's *haori*, then for *obijime*, and then for women's *haori*. Actual braids remaining from the Meiji period, however, are almost exclusively ones for men's *haori*.

Until later in the Meiji period, *obijime* seem to have been mostly stuffed cloth cords (*maruguke* and *hiraguke*), a continuation of Edo styles. It is only after the mid-Meiji period that, in both Tokyo and Iga almost simultaneously, kumihimo *obijime* began to be produced. During this mid-Meiji period, the Japanese government began to actively promote industry. Textile technology advanced; chemical dyes were imported, and silk kimono, which had previously been beyond the dreams of the working class, came to be within their means. After 1897, silk kimono as everyday wear began to be seen among the populace. This development gave birth to kumihimo used for *obijime*. At first they were fixed with metal buckles known as *pachin-dome*. Good quality *obijime*, however, appeared later, in the Taisho period (1912–1925).

14. Working at a *takadai*. In her right hand this worker holds a bamboo beater and with the left she exchanges the bobbin positions to form the interlacings of the braid.

Following the opening of Tokusaburo Hirosawa's factory, Iga kumihimo expanded steadily until, in 1904 with the Russo-Japanese War,
orders died out, creating a difficult period. After the war, business
conditions gained new vigor. The opening of the factory of my father,
Gen'ichi Nakauchi (brother-in-law of Tokusaburo Hirosawa), also
dates from this time. The trend towards old styles, which were popular at that time, spurred good business conditions and in turn activated
production in all areas of traditional Japanese clothing. The esteem for
the kimono exceeded preceding times: for example, even a person
supposed to have literary talent did not qualify as a man of letters
unless he had the education to describe lady's apparel in detail. Thus
Kyoka Izumi (1873–1939) in his Lady's Pedigree (Onna Keizu) lavishes
great detail and realism on depictions of gorgeous women's kimono.

From the end of Meiji into the Taisho period, Iga kumihimo
expanded around the circle of Tokusaburo Hirosawa's relatives and
friends. Evidence of its growing importance is the inclusion of braiding
on the marudai and of knotting (musubi) in the curriculum for girls
studying at the Mie Prefecture Tsu City Girls' High School. The rising
place of kumihimo gave birth to fashions and to the production of a
wide variety of cords. Although some of these were used as cords for
imported pocket watches and other nontraditional purposes, the production of kumihimo still centered on cords for obijime and haori.

After the Russo-Japanese War, with one or two exceptions, metal
buckles for obijime disappeared. (Even today the maiko entertainers
of Kyoto use buckles for their obijime for broad obi and buckles decorated with pearls or coral for the obijime used with narrower obi.)
During the Taisho period, interest changed to trying to bring alive the
quality of the braiding itself. In Iga, where the takadai, which is best
suited to producing pictorial designs, predominated, large quantities
of highly intricate obijime and haori cords were produced. While some
of the designs were old standbys, others were refreshing and new.
Some used conventionalized seasonal motifs—cherry blossoms for
spring, boats on a river for summer, chrysanthemums or maple leaves
for autumn, snowflakes for winter. Moving with the times, they also
braided designs of balls and bats to symbolize the famous Waseda/
Keio University baseball matches, and every year at New Year they
made cords with the theme of the poem composed by the emperor
for that year. Following the trends of the market, they found it necessary to accept orders for braids best done on the marudai, kakudai,
and ayatakedai. As a result, they called in craftsmen specialized in
braiding on those stands. When I was a child, a marudai craftsman
from Tokyo with the exacting temperament of an Edokko (native of
Edo—i.e., downtown Tokyo) came to live-in with us. I remember well
how one could calculate the time to the minute by the number of centimeters he had braided on the marudai.

From the Taisho period through the economic regulations preceding the Second World War, kimono and kumihimo prospered. New
styles of women's garb appeared, like visiting kimono and recreation
kimono. For obi, the more comfortable, lighter, narrower Nagoya obi
was devised to replace the broad, stiff brocade maruobi. Kumihimo

became wider: *haori* cords over one centimeter (one-half inch) wide and *obijime* three centimeters (one and one-half inches) wide. Color taste followed the fashions of the time: purple, vermilion, yellowish green, and contrasts of white and black, creating popular accessories that brought life to the texture of the braiding.

Modernization of the weaving industry due to electrification and mechanization accompanied the boom in kimono. In addition, synthetic silks such as rayon and nylon stimulated advances in yarn research and their practical applications. Because a similar mechanization did not advance kumihimo production, demand was met by increasing the number of women workers. Though a few worked in the factories, most worked at home. A visitor to Iga at that time could hear the sound of the beater of the *takadai* from every corner.

The great popularity of kumihimo as a home industry was due in part to the custom in Iga of keeping daughters close to their parents until marriage and discouraging apprenticeship or work away from home. There were, in fact, few places girls could find employment outside the house. Kumihimo-making appealed more than making straw ropes and sandals in that kumihimo braids are vastly more beautiful, and the technique was easier and drew a greater income than weaving. Daughters versed in braiding had special value as brides, so much so that, when they married, they generally brought along their braiding stands.

Iga products were not sold directly, but rather the craftsmen acted as subcontractors producing piecemeal for a fee and were dependent on wholesalers based in Kyoto, Kobe, and Osaka. The wholesalers placed orders for summer things in winter and winter things in summer. They held the products until they were ready to put them on the market, thus controlling the flow of goods. The braiders received dyed yarn and a specified order sheet from the wholesalers. They then strove to produce faster and cheaper than other places: the next order was decided on the quality of the finished product. This practice continued until the beginning of the economic regulations that followed World War II.

After the beginning of the Showa period (1925–), Japan saw increasingly darker economic conditions, such as the rice crash and growing unemployment. Despite this, the world of kumihimo continued its untroubled growth. Due to changes in fashion and in body size, the short cords for women's *haori*, which had been 13.5 centimeters ($5\frac{1}{3}$ inches) long increased to a length of 15 centimeters (6 inches).

Beginning in 1935, the military took over. In 1939 silk and rayon were rationed, price and standard controls instigated, and standardization of production began to overrule good quality. In 1940, due to the issuance of regulations on the making and selling of luxury items, most of the yarn was deflected to the making of parachutes and jumpsuits. Gold and silver threads were declared luxury items, not to be used for apparel. Among Iga workers, some toiled at extracting the gold and silver threads from cords they had completed in vain.

During the war period, braided cords were important for hanging medals on military uniforms. Braiders were kept busy making cords of ancient purple (*kodai murasaki*).

After the end of the war in 1945 till the economy began to recover from its collapse, the producers of kumihimo braided with materials dispensed from military coffers, such as parachute cords and cloth. Since throughout Japan commodities were very scarce, it was even possible to cut parachute cords into one-and-one-half meter (five feet) lengths, dye them, and sell them as kumihimo material. Since those cords were made of pure silk, which is easily handled when unraveled, even a novice could use them relatively simply. As a result, an increasing number of people turned to making kumihimo as a quick means of getting an income. Workers who before the war were content with producing for a fee with yarn supplied by wholesalers, now could buy raw materials. They thus began to make products of their own with their own silk.

The circumstances during this period in Iga and Tokyo differed fundamentally. While Tokyo saw two major disasters in the twentieth century—the great earthquake of 1923, which destroyed vast areas, and the Second World War bombings with shocking destruction (leading to general dispersion of craftsmen, who on return found no place waiting for them)—Iga, nestled in a valley far from any major military center, remained untouched by such physical devastation and could continue to provide work guarantees for its inhabitants. Thus, after the war Iga became the central place for the production of kumihimo.

As soon as the war troubles had settled, kimono regained popularity and saw a short boom period. *Obijime* became narrower, since fat ones were considered coarse, and designs became tempered, intended to blend with the design of the obi. Often braids were of one color only, their beauty being the braiding itself.

These circumstances led, in 1954, to the first introduction in Iga of iron machinery for braiding. Great effort was put into inventing a mechanical braider that would approximate hand braiding.

After 1955, when the Japanese economy outgrew its simple recovery and entered a period of expansion, Western clothing became the common garb. Kimono became "best clothes," resulting in a decline in demand for kumihimo. For a short time around 1970, kumihimo prospered again as a hobby, but being no longer essential to daily life, this amateur interest in kumihimo was unable to save the craft.

Today, the makers of Iga kumihimo cannot survive on making accessories for kimono alone. As a result, they have turned to more general uses for kumihimo in an effort to keep alive their precious art.

Translated by Monica Bethe

New Applications for Kumihimo

by Kei Sahashi

In the years following the Second World War, kumihimo have undergone a gradual decline. The reason lies solely in the limited uses for kumihimo since the Meiji period—as small accessories for traditional clothing (*haori* cords and *obijime*) (pages 68-71). The fate of kumihimo was thus bound up in the postwar decline of the kimono. Just as in the early Meiji period, the prohibition of carrying swords urged the kumihimo craftsmen to adapt their art to other uses, so, as a result of their being fewer and fewer kimono wearers, modern craftsmen must cultivate new fields. For the artisans, this provides a great test, but for those who have hopes that the world of kumihimo will expand as far as possible, it is most gratifying to think that from now on kumihimo will not be limited to *haori* cords and *obijime*, but will fit into many aspects of life and embellish living itself.

Today the greatest portion of kumihimo is produced in the city of Iga Uneo in Mie Prefecture. Kumihimo have, in fact, been designated the traditional craft of Iga (Pl. 15). The town is famous also as the birthplace of the renowned *haiku* poet, Matsuo Basho (1644-94) and the home of the father of No drama, Kan'ami Kiyotsugu (1333-84). About equally distanced from the three large cities of Kyoto, Osaka, and Nagoya, Iga has seen comparative prosperity since its early history (Pls. 16, 17).

From the Meiji period on, the kumihimo produced in this area (Pls. 18, 19) were made on order through wholesalers in Kyoto, the great producer and consumer of kimono. Until recently, therefore, it was more important to fulfill an order correctly than to apply imagination to the art of braiding. In the future, however, imaginative approaches to new uses of the tradition will become indispensable.

On these lines, the three people who have, in very different fields, done the most remarkable work are Junko Koshino, Minami Tada, and Hidejo Kanzaki. Coming from outside, this creative trio has sparked new life in the world of kumihimo.

In creating her works, fashion designer Junko Koshino (pages 14-

15. Illustrations of *Sixty-Some Celebrated Places* by Ando Hiroshige (1797–1858), showing Iga Ueno in the mid-nineteenth century. At the top of the road (upper left) is Iga Ueno Castle.

16. Iga Ueno Castle. Built by the lord of Iga, Todo Takatora, at the beginning of the seventeenth century in accord with orders from the first Tokugawa shogun, Ieyasu.

17. Samurai residences lining streets of Iga Ueno, where the atmosphere of the Edo period lingers.

18. *Obijime*, by Ken'ichi Fujibayashi. Silk and metallic thread. Produced on a *takadai*.

19. *Obijime*, by Takashi Fujioka. Silk and metallic thread. Produced on a *takadai*.

36) totally broke established conceptions of kumihimo. First, when she placed orders for kumihimo, she followed her own style, requesting untraditional colors and materials. She requested bold, strong colors—bright blue, green, yellow, and brown—which she used with and against black. Since none of her colors are found in the color sample books for traditional kumihimo, her orders afforded a refreshing surprise to the Iga kumihimo craftsmen.

Most epoch-making in the cooperative work between Koshino and the artisans was her insistence on the use of innovative materials. While silk was the standard traditional material, she proposed, as an experiment, that one of her designs be braided with fine metal wire. The surprised craftsmen found they could not produce the desired effects on standard braid stands or even on the existing iron machines. Their hands bled from braiding the hard metal.

The experiment, however, provided an extremely meaningful challenge. Now any number of new materials are being tried out. Belts braided from steel wires line tires, making industrial use of the strength and elasticity inherent in braiding. Silver and silver-plated threads are braided into accessory cords. In addition, experimentation is beginning on braiding artificial fibers such as dacron and nylon colored in the raw state. Others are thinking along the lines of braiding various wools, inspired by the cords from Peru and Bolivia (page 72).

Unlike Koshino, sculptor Minami Tada (pages 38–40) exploits the beauty of existing braids in creative and vigorous ways. Different from the accessories of professionals, however, her pendants and other objects aim at expressing the complex intricacies and intriguing quality of braiding by incorporating braids into art works of different media.

Hidejo Kanzaki (pages 10–12) has worked to broaden the stage for braided cords and to create a new atmosphere and feeling for kumihimo by constructively incorporating kumihimo and knots (*musubi*) into traditional Japanese ceremonies and rituals.

To expand on the possible practical and decorative uses for kumihimo one has only to be inspired by many of the things we live with and use everyday. I myself wear kumihimo neckties, belts, and shoulder bag straps. Kumihimo neckties (pages 28, 29 and Pls. 20, 21) tie very easily, and even by the end of the day, the knot does not loosen. Braids slung over the shoulder are practical in that they rarely slip off, and highly fashionable in that they can be made in various colors and styles.

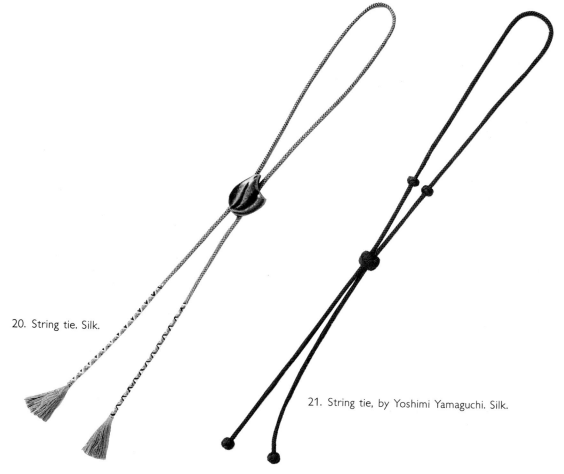

20. String tie. Silk.

21. String tie, by Yoshimi Yamaguchi. Silk.

Accessories (Pls. 22, 23) are an obvious outlet for kumihimo. Pendant and necklace cords and bracelets are probably most suitable. For interior design applications (Pls. 24–27), one might think of tapestries, space dividers, and fastening cords for rollup blinds or curtains. Kumihimo in single or varied colors and knots can be used as drawer pulls, lending a very elegant touch. Chair backs made with kumihimo have an elasticity that is comfortable. Other pleasing uses would be as tablecloths, table centers, lunch mats, and coasters (Pl. 28).

Though in this way the world of kumihimo has left the shelter of being a kimono accessory and broadened its horizons, even within the world of kimono, increasing experimentation is occurring. On the one hand, the new sense of design has affected the styles of *obijime* and *haori* cords. On the other, constructive innovation has produced new types of braids for traditional garments, for example men's obi and women's *zori* sandals of kumihimo (Pls. 29, 30). These are not only visually beautiful, but also fasten well, as those who have worn them testify.

22. Necklace, by Hitoshi Nakauchi. Silk and gold. Produced on the *omarudai* (large round stand).

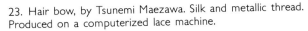

23. Hair bow, by Tsunemi Maezawa. Silk and metallic thread. Produced on a computerized lace machine.

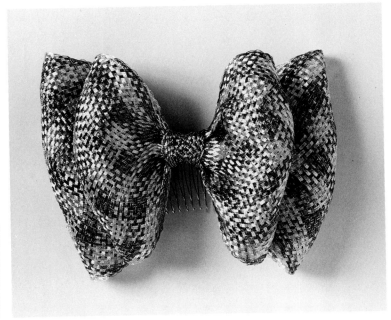

24. Kumihimo hanging, by Hitoshi Nakauchi. Silk. Produced on a *takadai*. W. 55.0 cm (21¾ in.), L. 210.0 cm (83⅓ in.).

25. Two kumihimo used as curtain cords. Produced on a *marudai*.

From now on, so that users can freely enjoy kumihimo, each according to his own taste, in addition to offering finished kumihimo products like neckties and necklaces, a good stock of different materials, variation of color, design, braiding methods, and numbers of bobbins should be made available. Furthermore, if one could buy kumihimo by length and width so as to suit ones own purposes, the usefulness of kumihimo would unquestionably increase.

In order for kumihimo to adapt to the times, braiders must not blindly follow the craft of the previous generations, but with enterprising minds that take tomorrow into account, they should endeavor to progress with originality. This, indeed, is the meaning of the words of the Iga-born poet Matsuo Basho when he said, "Without seeking the path of our ancestors, to pursue what they sought."

Translated by Monica Bethe

26. Decorative drawer pulls. Silk. Produced on a *marudai.*

27. Cords ornamenting a stool. Silk. Produced on a *kakudai*.

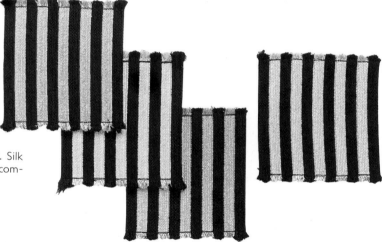

28. Coasters, by Seichu Maruyasu. Silk and metallic threads. Produced on a computerized lace machine.

29. Wide man's obi, by Koichi Hirosawa. Silk. Produced on a *takadai*.

30. *Zori* sandals and handbag, by Koichi Hirosawa.
Silk and metallic threads. Produced on a *takadai*.

31. Kumihimo dolls, figures of dancing lions, by Mizuki Inoue.
Silk. Produced on a *marudai*.

Notes to the Color Plates
Numbers refer to the pages on which the color plates appear.

1. A braid (the type known as *koraigumi*) partly completed on the *takadai*.

The six colors used here typify ancient colors of the eighth century such as are found in the Shoso-in: indigo blue, moss green, slightly reddish purple, off-white, rust, and golden brown. Among them, indigo has often been cited as the characteristic color of the Japanese people. In the eighth century the word for indigo, *ai*, referred to dyestuffs in general, so that the crimson dye produced from imported safflower was written as "dyestuff [*ai*] from China [*kure*]."

In early times the most primitive method of dyeing consisted of rubbing flowers or leaves directly onto a garment. The petals of the iris render a purplish blue color when treated this way. In the eighth century *Man'yoshu* anthology of poems, poem number 1361 refers to this dye process.

suminoe no	Robe rubbed with iris
asasawa ono no	growing in the ponds
kakitsubata	of Suminoe:
kinu ni suritsuke	When is the day
kimuhi shirazumo	it is to be worn?

Here the image of the iris also carries the meaning of a sweetheart, giving the poem an imbedded meaning of, "When shall I meet you as my wife?"

In the Nara period (701–794), they knew not only primitive rubbing techniques but also dye methods employing mordants, which both fix a dye and affect its shade. In order to dye a purple that was not too red and not too blue, for instance, yarn had to be treated with something containing both alum and with an alkaline content before immersing it in a bath extracted from the roots of the gromwell plant (*murasaki*). Lye taken from camellia ash turns out to have the perfect balance. The poem 3101 in the *Man'yoshu* discloses this dye secret. This poem, like the previous one, can be read also as a love poem with the word camellia acting as a pivot between the two halves.

Murasaki wa	To make purple,
haisasu mono zo	use camellia ash.
tsubakichi no	In camellia market
yaso no chimata ni	who is it stands
aeru ko ya tare	at the crossroads?

2–3. Yarn wound on large spools. The colors are ones used today. These threads are reserved for securing the tassels.

4. Bobbins hanging from a *takadai*. As a rule one bobbin weighs about 100 grams (roughly $\frac{1}{4}$ pound). Normally the greatest number of bobbins used to make one *obijime* (cord securing an obi) would be about seventy-four.

Hidejo Kanzaki
Hidejo Kanzaki is the head of the Kanzaki school of Japanese classical dance known as *jiuta mai*. The center of the transmitted art of these dances for women is the city of Kyoto. Choreographed to Ikuta school *jiuta* songs set to koto music, they were originally solo dances performed in banquet rooms without any props. Many of the *jiuta mai* are love dances. Hidejo states she would like her dances to express the heart of women living today.

Hidejo Kanzaki's success extends abroad. She has gained high acclaim for performances in various countries, including at the Art Festival in Avignon, France, and recently for a performance in the Opera House in Milan, Italy.

Her uses of kumihimo, like her dance, brim with heartfelt esteem for the beautiful forms of the past, yet the expression remains bright and fresh.

10. Kagami. This New Year's decoration of a rice offering in the form of rice cakes (*omochi*) is garnished with decorative ties made from kumihimo of seven colors, lending a touch of gayety to the solemnity of New Year's.

11. Tanabata Star Festival. Celebrated on July 7, this festival celebrates the legend about how the Princess Weaver Star (Vega) and the Cowherd Star (Altair), normally separated by the width of the Milky Way, meet as lovers on this night. Bamboo branches hung with handmade paper figures and talismans are the traditional decoration for the festival. Here the wishes normally written on talismans are expressed as decorative knots in kumihimo to produce a playful array of colors and knotted shapes.

Knots, in addition to their practical function, had a mystical and symbolic content.

In the Heian period (794–1192), the types of kumihimo and their meanings were codified along with other time-honored customs of the nobility. Decorative knots ornamented clothing and daily objects in many places. The ladies of the court, as a part of their cultural refinements, learned decorative knotting (hanamusubi) along with composing poems and playing instruments.

As times changed, and the warrior class came to dominate politics and society (twelfth century on), knots were used in the construction of armor and helmets. In addition, decorative knots found new uses among cultural pastimes such as incense-smelling and the tea ceremony. For example, the complicated knots of cords closing bags for tea utensils (Pl. 32) were kept as guarded secrets and had the purpose of sealing the bags so as to avoid possible surreptitious insertion of poisons or exchange of contents. The *Hoketsu no ki* (*Record of Knots and Wraps*) (Pl. 33),

which appeared in 1764, compiles examples of the various decorative knots of the warrior-class culture. It illustrates the use of some fifty types of knots. These include anything from paper string (*mizuhiki*) of red, black, and white for tying up parcels, to knots for cosmetic boxes, scroll pictures, and bags for halberds.

In this way the various knots (Pl. 34) that developed were cataloged. Over and above their practicality, these knots were rooted in the hearts of the people, who saw in them symbolic and spiritual meaning.

11. Tray for the ceremony of receiving a name (becoming a professionally recognized dancer). A soup made of greens, chicken, and thin noodles with kelp, dried squid, with pickled plums (*umeboshi*) on the side is served. The greens (*nappa*) and the chicken (*tori*) together spell NATORI (to receive a name). The kelp (*kobu*) symbolizes joy (*yorokobu*), and the dried squid, which tastes better the longer one chews it, suggests a long career—one that lasts "until one is wrinkled" (the appearance of pickled plum). The red color of the plum augurs a "lustrous" performance.

12. Dance. An experimental woman's dance based on *jiuta mai* but employing kumihimo as props and performed to modern music.

32. Decorative ties for tea utensil bags. Bags by Iwao Nukada, tie by Shoen Hashida. Bamboo leaf tie (left); chrysanthemum tie (right).

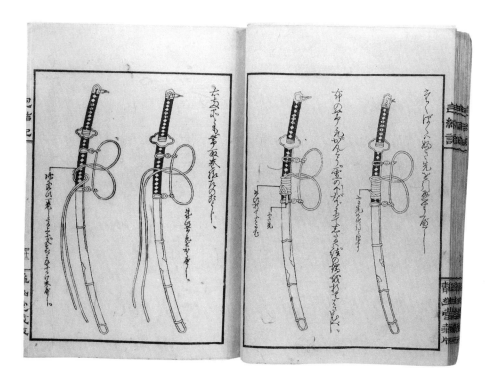

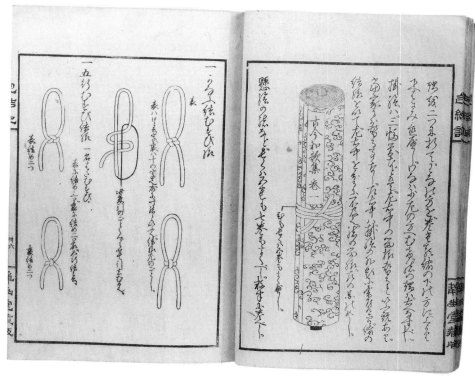

33. The *Hoketsu no ki* (*Record of Knots and Wraps*), 1840 copy. Owned by Yoshio Nakauchi.

A compilation of various knots by the mid-Edo period collector of customs of the nobility, Sadatake Ise (1715–84), respected also for his extensive knowledge of the institutions of the military class. Illustrated here are decorative knots for swords and practical ties for scrolls.

34. Various knots.
From upper left, *agemaki musubi, keman musubi, kiku musubi, kame musubi,
tsuru musubi, renzoku awabi musubi.*

Junko Koshino

One of the most active fashion designers today, Junko Koshino works as a total coordinator on a broad scale. She moves freely from costume design for stage and movies to designing uniforms, everyday clothes, and interiors. Her activities extend overseas: shops in Paris, Milan, Beijing, and Taipei have won her high acclaim.

About kumihimo, Koshino comments, "The universe is created completely of rounds. Kumihimo are objects formed into rounds by the hands of people. I have tried to base my creations on the image of that master plan of rounds."

14–15. Spiral
16–17. White and black curtain cords
18. Turban
19. Turban with fringe
20. Earrings: "Whirlpool"
Bracelet: "Horizon"
21. Necklace: "Ripples"
22. "Jive"
23. "Shift"
24. Cords for small objects
25. "Gloves"
26. Belts with interlaced colors
27. "Bag to the Future"
28–29. Shirts and ties
30–31. Red and black corded jackets
32–35. Kimono sets: "Japan Style"
36. Lacquer ware

Minami Tada

Minami Tada is a representative modern Japanese sculptor. Using materials such as acrylic, glass, and stainless steel, she opens new fields in the world of three-dimensional constructions. Her work includes not only pure sculpture, but also designs using lighting effects and architectural space constructs. All her pieces are highly esteemed.

Minami Tada's connection with kumihimo stretches far back. Ever since she first felt the magic of kumihimo, she has collected them with the intention of sometime incorporating braided cords into her works. In particular, kumihimo combine well with her works in glass. The complex interlacings of the kumihimo harmonize well with the infinite varieties of light changes in her glass creations, each bringing out the beauty of the other.

38. Glass and kumihimo
39. Glass pendants with kumihimo
40. Glass pendants and stone pendant with kumihimo

Historical Illustrations

65. Hanging ornament. Karakumi braid with gilt-bronze bells. Asuka period. W. 55 cm (c. 2¼ in.). Important Cultural Property. Tokyo National Museum Horyji Treasure Hall.

This braid, owned by Empress Suiko (593–628), is said to be a decoration for a screen or room curtain. The base color, madder red, remains vibrant even today. The harmony of the red with the touches of gold and black and the ornamental bells suggests that the piece is probably an import from the continent. If not imported, it certainly is the work of an immigrant craftsman.

This flat braid with diamonds composed of Vs done alternately in mirror image is known as a "double diamond Chinese braid" (futahishi no karakumi). Since the diamonds are long and thin, it is thought to have been braided on a karakumidai, a stand for braiding Chinese braids.

In later years the hirao, the flat decorative sash used with formal court dress, developed from karakumi braids.

65. Brocade sutra cover for the Issai-kyo sutra. Flat braid, gold butterfly fasteners. Late Heian period. W. 2.0 cm (c. 1.0 in.). Important Cultural Property. Formerly the property of Jingo-ji temple, Kyoto.

A complete set of sutras was dedicated by Retired Emperor Goshirakawa (1156–1158, died 1192) to Jingo-ji temple in Takao, north of Kyoto. The sutras are divided into ten-volume units, each of which is rolled into a cover made of bamboo slats held together with decorative plaiting and flat braided cords attached in a Y shape. Since the braiding is very loose, it is thought this was made solely by finger manipulation, without a stand.

66. Cords for brocade-wrapped talismans. National Treasure. Rectangular braid, 1.0 cm × 0.5 cm (c. $\frac{3}{8} \times \frac{1}{8}$ in.). Late Heian period. Shitenno-ji temple, Osaka.

This was an amulet worn over the chest by women on pilgrimage to a temple or shrine. Brocade cloth wraps the form made from Japanese cypress. The cords are 4 rib by 6 rib rectangular braids thought to have been made with finger loop techniques rather than on a stand with bobbins. Special braiding techniques have kept the edge threads so that they remain at the edge and do not pass through the center ribs, becoming a part of the overall pattern, as is usual for most square or rectangular braids.

66. Hirao sashes.

Upper: Hirao sash, karakumi braiding. Blocks of purple and white with embroidered design of long-tailed birds. Flat kumihimo, W. 8.4 cm (3⅓ in.), L. 264 cm (104¾ in.). Each tassel 26.0 (10⅓ in.)

Middle: Hirao sash, karakumi braiding. Blocks of yellowish green and white with embroidered design of characters from a poem found in the Man'yoshu. Flat braid, W. 8.0 cm (3 in.), L. 257.0 cm (102 in.). Each tassel 23.0 cm (9 in.).

Bottom: Hirao sash, karakumi braiding with embroidered design of flocks of magpies and peonies. Flat braid, W. 8.4 cm (3⅓ in.), L. 209.0 cm (83 in.). Each tassel 23.0 cm (9 in.).

All three are Edo period pieces owned by Hisashi Oomichi. Photo by Tsunehiro Kobayashi.

Beginning in the Heian period, formal dress for the nobility consisted of the sokutai costume of broad-sleeved cloak with baggy pants and black lacquered hats. Part of the stipulations for this costume, according to the rules of ancient customs, was to have hirao decorative sashes with long end tassels bind the cloak at the waist, their ends forming a central dangling panel. Only nobles of a rank above five could wear hirao braided in karakumi technique, and these came to symbolize their authority. The delicate designs and color combinations of hirao sashes as well as their fine braiding exemplify the height of kumi-himo art.

The precision of the diamonds, the arrangement of the shading of the colors of the *hirao* seen here reflect Japanese rather than Chinese taste.

67. Cords with tortoiseshell pattern (hexagons) on two surfaces.

National Treasure. Rectangular cord, 1.4 cm x 0.5 cm ($\frac{1}{2}$ x $\frac{1}{8}$ in.). Heian period. Kumano Hayatama Shrine, Wakayama Prefecture. Photo by Tsunehiro Kobayashi.

The cord shown here is one of six preserved by the shrine. The use of this rectangular braid of 4 ribs by 8 ribs is unclear. Probably it was made by loop braiding techniques with four people working together, each person manipulating 18 loops, 9 per hand.

67. Red-laced armor. National Treasure. Kamakura period. Kushibiki Hachiman-gu shrine, Aomori Prefecture. The splendid, extremely exquisite gold ornamentation shows the brilliance of the goldwork of the late Kamakura period. The body of the armor is also elaborate. According to shrine tradition, the piece was dedicated by Emperor Chokei (1343-94).

The lacing braids are single flat cords, while the helmet cords are not braids, but stuffed cloth cords. The belt cord is a thick, flat braided cord with hexagon pattern on one side only. The edging cords along the skirt also have hexagons on one side of a flat braid. This piece of armor was stolen from the shrine just before World War II. After the war, it was recovered and repaired. The gold ornaments are the original Kamakura period pieces.

Iga braids and foreign braids

68-69. *Obijime* made in Iga. These double-weave *obijime* were made between the beginning of the Showa period (1925) and World War II. Double-weave construction consists of one braid composed of a back and front layer of flat braids. The threads from the back layer, when brought to the front for individual interlacings, create concrete, detailed designs. The braids shown here are typical of Iga and made on the *takadai*.

70-71. *Haori* cord made in Iga. These flat braids for fastening the front of the *haori* coat were made during the Taisho period (1912-1925) or in the early years of the Showa period (1925-). There are various kinds, including single-layer cords, double-weave cords, wide cords, and narrow ones. Both the braids inside the box and those outside are women's *haori* cords. Today following western taste, the tendency is to match the color of the *haori* cord with that of the *haori*. Many *haori* cords made fifty years ago, however, had assertive colors and designs.

72. Peruvian slings and festive cords. Courtesy of Makiko Tada. These slings for throwing stones were used in warfare and hunting. The stones are placed in the wider central section with the crack, then the sling is folded in half. Holding the two ends of the cord, one swings it around, then releases one end to let the stone fly out.

These slings are entirely finger-braided—no stand is employed. One hand serves in place of the *marudai*, holding a number of threads of wool (sheep, alpaca, etc.). The other hand then exchanges the positions of the threads to create the braid. Since wool, unlike silk, does not slip easily, there is no need for weights, and one can simply tighten the braiding at each step as one progresses. The cradle section is woven.

Compared to the Bolivian slings shown below, the colors of the Peruvian slings are quieter, mostly the undyed natural colors of the wool.

The cords with colorful balls attached are dance accessories used at festival time.

72. Bolivian stone throwing slings. Courtesy of Makiko Tada. The basic techniques and materials used to make these slings are the same as those for Peruvian slings. The cradles, however, are done in *karakumi* technique, without the use of a stand. The bright colors are made with vegetable dyes and cochineal. Today few people can braid cords as fine as these.

Translated by Monica Bethe

新しい組紐の世界

佐橋 慶編

目　次

紐とこころ

大岡　信

　「ひも」という語の語源は何だったかについては幾通りもの説があり、定説とするに足るほどのものはないようである。しかし中で最も私に興味深く思われるのは、ミクロネシアその他の民族誌研究家であり言語学者であった松岡静雄の説である。すなわち彼は、「ひも」は「秘緒」の約だという。「下着の紐は神秘なものとして夫婦の間がらの外は決して他人に手を触れしめなかった」と彼は『日本古俗誌』の中で書いている。

　主として七世紀半ばから八世紀半ばまでの和歌を集めて成った『万葉集』の中には、松岡の説く意味での紐への神秘的信仰にもとづく男女の恋歌がたくさん含まれている。

　仮に「ひも」が「秘緒」の語のつづまったものであるかどうか不確かであるとしても、日本人が古代から、紐というものにきわめて深い精神的な意味を見出してきた民族であることは、疑いがない。紐は「結ぶ」ことを本質とする。すべての秘すべき大切なものを包みこみ、守ってゆくこと、それが紐の機能であり、また象徴的意味である。したがって、紐は物体をくくりつけ、結び合わせるだけではなく、心をくくりつけ、結び合わせる行為を象徴するものとなる。古代の愛し合う男女は、契りを結んだあと、別れにのぞんで互いの衣服の紐を結び合い、次に逢うまでは解かないことを誓い合った。これを再び解く時は、身も心も相手に棒げて、何の分け隔てもなく心から打ち解けることを意味していた。

　紐を結ぶことは、いわば結ぶ人の命をそこに籠めることをも意味していたから、相手に対する愛の告白にもなったし、またその健康や安全を祈ることにもなった。このことは、人類共通のしぐさとして、神や仏に祈るとき、人々が合掌し、指を組み合わせるという事実をも思いおこさせる。

　占いその他の呪術が、まだ強い磁力をもって人々の生活を支配していた日本の王朝文化の時代が、同時に紐芸術の一大発達の時代であったことは当然である。紐は吉凶、占いの意味を持ち、また男女の性別をも意味するものとして、その切口の形状や太い細いの別、多様な色彩、想像を絶するほどに豊富なスタイルの結び方等によってその用途を果たした。ここでは実用性と装飾性は互いに相乗的効果をもって緊密に結びついていた。

王朝の貴婦人たちの衣服や調度品を飾っていた紐も、中世武士の鎧兜の各所を結びつけていた紐も、実用的で同時に装飾的、呪術的で同時に象徴的であるという本質を共有していた。この本質はその後もずっと、現代にいたるまで日本の紐飾りの中で保たれ続けている。

　私はかつて京都のある尼寺の庵主さんから、日本の飾り緒結びには一千種類ほどの結び方があっただろうと考えられるという話を聞かされ驚嘆したことがある。彼女はそう言ったあとこう付け加えて私を再び仰天させた。

　「わたくしはまだ百種類ぐらいしか作れないのです、おはずかしいことでございますが」

　あとで私は、この庵主さん西垣琳弘尼が、古代からの飾り緒結びの復元に甚大な功績のある研究家であり、実践を通じてその伝統を甦えらせつつある作家であることを知った。

　紐は今なお、人々の心をそのようにして結びつける力を持っているのだった。

組紐の歴史

多田牧子

周知のとおり、日本ではかなり古くから紐を、とりわけ組紐を多用している。しかしそれにもかかわらず、何故私たちが〝紐の文化〟をもつに至ったのか明瞭に答えることはむつかしい。何時、誰が、何のために、どのようにして組紐をもたらしたのか、そしてそれはどのように発展し、そこにはどんな技術が隠されているのか、多くの疑問点を残している。

組紐を解明しようとするとき、いくつかの障碍に出くわす。それは、まず組紐が大変朽ちやすい素材でできているため、残存する遺品がとても少ないこと。次に、組紐は、その性質上主役になることはなく、何かに付属、付帯するものであるため、本体なり主役なりが保存されていても、付属品である組紐は交換されたり失なわれていることが多いこと。さらに、難しい組み方など技術は、口伝、秘伝であったため記録がほとんどなく、従って推量によらざるを得ないことなどがそれである。

以上の様々な疑問点を少しずつ解きほぐしながら、想像力をたくましくして、組紐やその歴史を辿ってみたい。

組紐とは何か？

紐には、裁(たち)紐・撚(より)紐・絎(くけ)紐・束(たばね)紐・編紐・織紐・組紐があり、それぞれの特性を生かした用途に使いわけられている。

組紐が他の紐と違う点は、３つ以上の糸又は糸束が、斜めに交差して、すでに紐ができ上がっている方向とは常に逆の方へ糸（又は糸束）が動いてできるというところにある。その特長は、組み方や手加減で、用途にあわせた伸縮性や強度を持たせることができ、物を緊縛するのに適している点にある。

組紐を大まかに分類すると、丸組紐（角組紐）と平組紐に分けられる。

丸組紐は撚紐から発展したもので、基本は丸四つ組である。丸四つ組は、糸の動きを分解すると、次の図の様になるが、①のみをくり返すと右撚りの紐、②のみをくり返すと左撚りの紐ができる。したがって右撚りと左撚りが交互に行なわれてできた紐が組紐である。これは１人でも、もちろん道具なしでできるが、太いものを作る時などは２人で作ったとも考えられる。

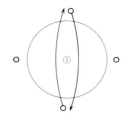 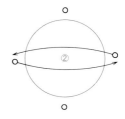

平組紐の祖ともいうべきは三つ組で、条数がふえたり、糸の運びが複雑になって発展していく。組紐の組織の発展の方法は、また単位の連結によってもできる。たとえば、唐組が一菱→二菱……十菱→十三菱と横方向につながったり、角組→御岳組→西大寺組・中尊寺組→四天王寺の懸守の紐→両面亀甲のように連結して素晴しい組紐ができる。

なぜ日本は紐の文化を持っているのか？

日本では古来、「結ぶ」ということに精神的、神秘的、呪術的な意味があり、それゆえ紐の文化が発展したと考えられる。

紐は、仏事、武具、装束などと深くかかわっており、日本人ほど物を結ぶ民族はほかに類をみないであろう。かつて騎馬民族系の留め方である「入れ紐」という、いわばボタンが伝えられたが、結局平安末期には形式的に用いられるだけとなり相変わらず結びが多用された。

組紐は、こうした中で特に服飾の体系と深くかかわり重要な役割もってきた。現在ではそれが帯締めに代表されている。帯締めは帯を締め上げ、きもの全体のアクセントとなるなどきものの最後の仕上げをしている。

ここで洋服ときものを比較してみると、洋服は立体構造なので、その中に身体を入れるだけでよく、ボタン、ホック、ファスナーなどを用い規定性の強い留め方をする。従って個人的である。一方きものは、直線的、平面的で、裁断は画一的、身体に巻きつけるだけで誰にでも合わせることができ、フリーサイズとさえ言えるものである。

そして、きものは「結び」という任意性、融通性に富む留め方で形づくられる。季節、気候に合わせ、あるいは、着て行く場所、個人の好みに応じてきつくもゆるくも自由に着ることができる。「紐」や「結び」に対する精神的な意味のほかに、それらがもつ融通性が日本人の生活風土にとても馴染みがよかったため、それらはわが国独特の発展をしてきたと考えられる。

なぜ紐があらわれたか？[縄文・弥生それ以前]

原始時代、人間が何かを身にまとい始めた時、何かを束ねて持とうとした時、何かをつなごうとした時から、紐は人間が考え出した知恵であった。それは多分世界中のあちこちで必要にせまられて考え出されたのであろう。しかし、紐とそれを結ぶことによって簡単化された仕事を思うと、注目すべき人知と言えるだろう。

それは最初は、植物のつるや動物の皮をさいたものであったと思われるが、徐々に強さを増すために本数（条数）をふやし、撚りをかけ、そして交差して組まれるようになったと考えられる。

紀元前10,000年頃、日本には縄文文化と呼ばれる時期があった。竪穴式住居に住み、装飾のほどこされた土器を持ち狩猟・漁労・採集による生活を営んでいた。

この時代にまさに紐の痕跡がある。それは土器に紐を圧しつけた圧痕文である。撚紐やあるいは撚紐を棒に巻きつけたものを、土器の表面に転がしてつけたと思われる。

では、なぜ縄文を土器につけたのだろうか？撚紐や撚紐棒を転がすことによって土がしまると考えたのだろうか。あるいは、紐が「細くて長く、柔軟性に富んでいて、継ぐことで長く延長でき、結ぶことで物を束ねたりできる」といった性質をもつことから、紐の呪術性を多収穫豊穣として願いをこめ、この文様をつけたのかも知れない。縄文が豊穣を願う土偶にも施されていることを考えると紐は神秘的に取り扱われていたように思える。

丸紐の原型である丸四つ組の回転圧痕は、飛鳥山公園内貝塚（東京都北区王子）出土の片口付深鉢と上福岡貝塚（埼玉県入間郡福岡町）出土の片口付深鉢に認められる。平紐の原型の三つ組は、北海道草創期東釧路式の壺に圧痕が認められた。又、ひもが元のままの姿で出土したものもある。福井県の鳥浜貝塚から出たもので、それらは土器面に文様をつけるための原体になったものや、住居の丸太を縛ったもの、漁労や狩猟につかわれたものと考えられている。

少し下って弥生式文化になると紐の圧痕文は土器から消える。これはろくろを使って大量生産をしたからと思われる。しかしこの時代は水稲耕作を始めた時代でもあるし紐類を多用していたであろう。

その弥生時代の中期、当時の日本が、『後漢書東夷伝』の中に引見される。「建武中元二年（西暦57年）倭奴国　貢を奉げて朝貢す使人自ら大夫と称す　倭国の極南界なり　光武賜うに印綬を以てす」と記されている。漢の帝室は、「内臣」や「外臣」とよばれる属国の首長に一定規格の印綬をさずけその地位を保障したのである。綬とは、中国で官職の印を帯びるに用いた組紐のことである。(広辞苑)その印とされるものが、博多湾の志賀島で1784年に発見された。それは「漢委奴国王」と刻まれた金印で、蛇鈕を持つ。鈕とは、印または鏡などのつまみ、多くは紐を通す孔があるものを言う。(広辞苑)どんなにか美しい組紐がこの印についていたのか想像するのは楽しいものである。

弥生後期の３世紀頃の日本は『魏志倭人伝』でわかる。239年卑弥呼の女王国は、大夫の難升米を帯方郡（朝鮮半島の北西部）、ついで魏の都洛陽に送り、10人の生口と二匹二丈の班布をささげた。それに応えて魏の明帝は銀印青綬をさずけた。また銅鏡100枚交龍錦、紺地句文錦などとりどりのものもさずけられている。倭人伝には上記の他に「綬」の字が２個ほど見られる。このようにして、大陸との往来が始まり、自力で作っていた紐の文化に加えて、大陸の紐の文化が入り影響を与えたと考えられる。

古墳文化の組紐は？［大和時代］

３世紀末から４世紀末頃の間は、謎の世紀といわれる。大和朝廷の起源、つまり天皇の起こりとでもいうものや、朝鮮半島への進出など、きわめて重要なことが多いにもかかわらず、『魏志倭人伝』のような詳細な史実の記録がないからである。『古事記』『日本書記』では、神話を歴史化した部分があると思われるからである。

そこで、先ず古墳について見てみよう。３世紀末から７世紀まで古墳文化が栄えた。この時代は前・中・後期と区別され、中期に古墳は最大規模になり、後期は小規模の群集墳となる。この古墳の副葬品から当時の様子をうかがうことができる。

それらは、鏡・玉などの呪術宝器、馬具や武具、土師器、須恵器、家・動物・人物などを表わす形象埴輪である。伊賀の久米山古墳から青銅鏡が発掘された折、そのひとつの裏面の鈕に朱色の角紐と思われるものがついていたが空気にふれて灰となってしまったそうである。このように紐は材料が風化しやすく現在まで残存するものが無いのは残念なことである。

　ところで、埴輪をみると紐が多く用いられていたことがわかる。美豆良（みずら）を結う紐、衣服のための胸紐・腰紐・足結（あゆい）の紐などがそうである。それらはどの種類の紐であったかはわからないが、紐がしっかりと生活の中に根づいていたことをしのばせる。（１図参照）紐を結ぶことによって、悪いものが中に入ってこないように、又魂が外に出ていかないようにと考えられていたのかも知れない。

　400年頃、応神天皇の時代に有名な帰化人の伝説がある。阿知使主（あちのおみ）と弓月の君の話である。阿知使主は、漢氏の祖で、多くの手工業技術者を百済・南朝からつれてきて管理する役目を果たしたと思われる。このころ大和朝廷は、勢力が強く百済を属国視し、さかんに技術者を呼びよせ朝廷の手工業組織の中に組み入れていたようである。弓月の君も百済から多数の人を引きつれて渡来し、養蚕や機織の新技術を伝えたと考えられており、秦氏の祖といわれる。この時、組紐の技術が入って来たかどうかは定かではない。

　また、562年大伴狭手彦が高句麗に行って織物、組紐を持ち帰り、しかも組紐職人を連れて来たとも伝えられている。この年は、朝鮮半島にあった日本政府の拠点、任那日本府（みまな）が新羅に滅ぼされた年であるから、救援に向った狭手彦が職人たちを連れて帰国したのかも知れない。

唐組は唐から来たのか？［飛鳥時代］

　538年、仏教の伝来とともに仏教で比較的重要な役割を持つ紐も付随して入って来たと思われる。飛鳥文化は、聖徳太子が奨励した仏教を基調とした貴族本位の文化である。また渡来人中心の大陸模倣文化とも言える。遣隋使・遣唐使を中国に送り、中国を通じて遠くギリシャへもつながっており国際性は豊かだった。

　この時代、607年に建立された法隆寺には素晴しい組紐が残されている。現在は東京国立博物館に保存されているこれらの組紐は、この当時、日本で組まれたものか、中国から渡って来たものか、わからない。しかしその高度な技術と大陸的なくっきりとした色使いは、中国のものと思われる。（日本は舶来物を良しとして、いいものは唐物や韓物といわれることが多かったのではあるが。）

　この時代の代表的な遺品には次のようなものがある。

　「幡縁飾組紐（ばんのへりかざり）」（２図参照）東京国立博物館保管の法隆寺献納宝物。強い撚りの糸でＶ字（矢羽）模様に組み出した、いかにも大陸的な配色の力強い紐。仏教で用いる幡という旗の縁飾りに使用されていた。組み方は、後年「笹浪組（さきなみ）」と呼ばれるものである。この縁飾は糸の交差角度がかなり鋭角である点から、古い型の組台である唐組台かそれに似た台（たとえば、枝や枠に糸を掛け、落ち着かせる場所に刻みや木くぎを立てたもの）を使用して組まれたと考えられる。あるいは指に糸をかけて組むループ操作法（後述）によったのかも知れない。この組紐と同種の組紐が白鳳時代（８世紀頃）に描かれた聖徳太子像の太刀の帯に見られる。

　「金銅装唐組垂飾（こんどうそうからくみすいしょく）」（65頁左参照）、やはり法隆寺の献納宝物。推古天皇の几帳（きちょう）の垂飾として使われていたと言われる。菱の形が縦方向に細長く、唐組台が用いられたと考えられる。この紐は、正倉院の組紐より後のものではないかとする説も

あるが、色使い、金銅の飾りや鈴などから、この時期に舶載されたか帰化人によって作られたものと思われる。

「玉帯」、一間組（安田組）で玉を組み込んである。これも唐組台で比較的きれいに組むことができる。しかし当時どのようにして組まれたかは定かではない。

以上のほかに、この時代、701年の大宝律令、718年の養老律令の衣服令により衣服が厳しく規定され男子の礼服には条帯が用いられた。これは一間組で、なかには真珠やガラス玉が組み込まれたものもあったというから、法隆寺に残された玉帯のようなのものであったろう。

正倉院の組紐を作った道具は？［奈良時代］

アジア大陸に栄えた古代文化がシルクロードを通って日本にやってきた。シルクロードの終着点と言われる正倉院には数々の遺品が保存されている。（3図参照）

なかでも組紐は唐からのもの、又は唐文化の影響を受けたものがたくさん残されている。

正倉院の組紐の中には一間組・二間組・三間組・四間組・二条軸一間組（笹浪組）・角組など、現在の組紐の原型がほとんど残されている。その内訳は、354例中一間組…47例、二間組…11例、三間組…9例、四間組…8例、二条軸一間組…12例、角組…240例、一間丸組…4例、四条組…1例、撚紐…21例、他…1例。

また一番多い角組の条数は240例中、10条…1例、12条…14例、14条…109例、16条…60例、18条…50例、20条…4例、不明…2例である。

ところで、これらの組紐は、どのようにして組まれたのであろうか？　何か道具を使ったのだろうか？

近年、組紐研究家の木下雅子氏はこれらの組紐はループ操作法で組まれたのではないかとの説を出しいる。ループ操作法とは、糸端におもり玉をつけるのではなく、ループ（輪）にして、そのループを指や手に掛けて持ち左手左端の糸が右手左端へ、右手右端の糸が左手右端へというように移動して組まれる組み方である。正倉院の組紐の場合、特に角組に注目すると、4の倍数条の組紐は78例、4の倍数条ではない組紐が160例見られる。4の倍数条ではない組紐（つまり奇数の2倍の組組）は、丸台のような道具を用いても組めるが、ループ操作法の方がすんなりと効率よく組める。またループ操作法では平たい紐も組める。

以上のことから、先ず、この時代の紐は道具なしで、単に指の操作のみで作られたと考えるのが妥当と思われる。使ったとしても、ループ操作をした後で打ちこむための足打台（4図参照）のようなものであろう。ただし平紐類は、ループ操作法で美しく組むのは難しい。法隆寺の組紐の項で述べた唐組台の様なもので組んだとすると、二条軸一間組の矢羽の角度も同じ位であるし、一間組などもきれいにでき上がる。

ともかくも、正倉院の組紐はいずれも素晴らしいものばかりで、正倉院は、まさに組紐の宝庫である。

組紐はどのように進化したか？［平安時代と鎌倉時代］

奈良時代は唐文化の影響をもろに受けた時代であった。平安時代の前半期までその傾向が続く。というよりもむしろもっと唐文化的であったかも知れない。そして後半期は、唐文化を消化しつくし、日本独自の道を歩く文化となった。

そのきっかけは、894年菅原道真の提唱によって遣唐使が廃止されたことにある。

廃止の理由は、唐が衰退してきたこと、航海の危険、財政の困難などである。しかし、我が国では前述したように唐の文化を吸収してしまい国風文化に移る気運があったことが見逃せない。

組紐の分野でももちろん同一の道を歩み、純粋に日本的な組紐が作られるようになる。その例としてまず、平緒をあげることができる。この時代、男子の礼服は束帯であるが、袍(ほう、表衣、うえのきぬ)の色が位により定められていた。四位以上が黒、五位が蘇枋(赤紫系)、六位は縹(藍色系)であった。そこで身分の高い四位以上の人々は黒袍で趣向をこらせるのは平緒しかなかった。平緒にも規定があり、五位以上は唐組、六位以下は絁(かんばた、織紐)又は新羅組とあった。いきおい高位の人々は、優雅な唐組平緒で美しさを競ったようである。(66頁下参照)

この唐組平緒は法隆寺に残された二菱唐組が日本的に発展したもので、巾の両端に濃い色や小菱をあしらう。また、中央部分を段染めにした糸で組み上げた紫緂、櫨緂、棟緂などもあり、鳥や紋などの刺繍をほどこす。

京くみひもは、このような公家組紐の流れを祖にもつ。唐組平緒は有職の紐として、現在でも作られている。唐組平緒を代々造り伝えた深見家が京都にあり、その13代目の深見重助氏(1885〜1974)は組紐界でただ1人の人間国宝である。氏の仕事は、鷹司誓玉氏の『唐組平緒』に記され、古澤裕司氏、木下和子氏に受け継がれている。人間用の平緒は十菱、神様用(伊勢神宮のご神宝)は十三菱と有職で定められ、伊勢神宮のものは、現在でも20年に1度の式年遷宮の折に作りかえられている。

この唐組平緒と対照的に発達したものに肉厚で立体的な一連の連結角組がある。角組を2個連結して二連角組(御岳組)が、またそれが2個連結して四連角組(西大寺経巻錦袋の紐、中尊寺金色堂藤原秀衡の棺納入の組紐、鞆淵八幡宮神輿の総角の紐)が、さらに連結して六連角組(四天王寺懸守の紐、2種類)と発展する。(66頁上参照)これはさらにもう一歩進んで、鎌倉時代の八連角組(両面亀甲組)へと進化する。この考え方は道明の山岡一晴氏が大成した。

これらの連結角組は長い間、なぞの紐であった。しかし、木下雅子氏(正倉院の項参照)がループ操作法で見事に解明した。筆者も、木下氏の「両面亀甲もループ操作法で組めると思う」の言葉に従って試して見たがなるほど、スイスイと組めてしまうのである。多分、当時の人も、七十一番職人歌合絵巻や川越喜多院にある国宝職人尽図にあるような「足打台」を用いたり、打ちこむ人は別で横に2人、3人、4人と並んで連結させながらこれらの紐を組んだに違いない。なお組紐の老舗道明では、約2メートルの大丸台での復元に成功している。

では、中尊寺金色堂から藤原秀衡のミイラとともに出た紐について見てみよう。この当時の陸奥の金の産出量は、ぼう大なものであったらしい。奥州の藤原氏は、そうした土地を支配し栄華をきわめ、都の文化をどんどん取り入れ豪華きわまる生活をしたようだ。この特別な紐も、都から取り寄せたか、職人を連れてきて作らせたのであろう。その組み方は秘伝で、もし何かに記されたとしても、江戸時代の『止戈枢要』にあるように、一種の暗号を用いられていたと思われる。

なお両面亀甲組は、紀州熊野速玉大社(67頁左参照)、武州御岳神社(1280年鎌倉幕府七代将軍惟康親王が奉納した大鎧の繰締緒といわれる)、三島大社(1180年頃、源頼朝の妻北条政子が奉納した手箱の紐という)の三ヵ所に残されている。

両面亀甲組はまた江戸時代に、真野家平安重により復元されている。その紐を見た時どうも高台で組んだようなので、高台で組めないものかと考えた末やってみる

と、ループ操作法と同じ内部組織を持つものが、もっと簡単に手間も少なく組める
ことがわかった。これは非常に楽しい作業であった。

　ほかに、この時代特筆すべき組紐に、平清盛(1118～1181)が厳島神社に奉納した
経巻の紐(平家納経の厳島組)がある。優美で繊細な紐で気品がある。これは五代
目道明新兵衛氏が明治中期に復元に成功している。

　そして、この時代、忘れてはいけないものは「鎧」であろう。平安時代は美しい
組紐をふんだんに使った華麗な大鎧を作り出した。そして鎌倉時代にその最盛期
に入る。大鎧は紐を大量に使って作り上げられた芸術品、まさに紐工芸の集大成
といった観がある。

　代表的なものに、武州御岳神社の畠山重忠奉納の鎧、惟康親王奉納の鎧、大山
祇神社紺糸威鎧、猿投神社樫鳥糸威鎧などがある。このほか鎌倉末期の特徴をよ
く示し、豪華な装飾金具で飾られた櫛引八幡宮赤糸威鎧(67頁参照)、春日大社赤
糸威鎧はともによく知られている。

組紐は衰退したか？[室町時代から江戸初期]

　平安時代、鎌倉時代に頂点に登りつめたとされる組紐は、室町時代に入ると下
降の一途をたどったと考えられがちであるが、はたしてそうであろうか？何ごと
も、複雑なものがこれでもかこれでもかと続いた後は、なにかシンプルなものの
方が目新しいのではないだろうか？この時代、茶道がさかんになったのもこんな
ところに理由があるかも知れない。「わび・さび」の思想は、渋い色、より素朴簡潔
な組みへと紐をみちびいた。組紐の低迷期といわれるのにもかかわらず、消費量
は増加しているのである。

　応仁の乱(1467～1477)以後、長い戦乱のため、手間のかかる大鎧が作られなく
なり実用性の高いものへと変ってきたこともシンプルな組みを生んだ要因のひと
つである。組紐をはやく、きれいに組むために丸台、綾竹台、高台などの道具も
考え出されたようである。(6、10、12図参照)

　簡単に簡単にと動いたこの時代は、たしかに組紐の組織の高度化や、いわゆる
名品の出現はなかったが、組紐の需要が貴族階級、武士階級から庶民へと巾が広
がり、人々の生活により密着してきた時代といえると思う。

　16世紀半ば、織田信長(1534～1582)豊臣秀吉(1538～1598)により天下が統一さ
れ、長い戦乱の時代は終る。これが安土桃山時代で、美術工芸が再び栄え始めた。
この時代の文化の特長は、新興大名や都市の豪商をにない手として豪壮・華麗で
たくましいことである。しかも庶民的であり、人間中心の文化と感じられる。組
紐の分野でも、この気運はたかまり、戦国時代の実用的なものから、遊び心のあ
るものへと変化していった。そして、鎧師の兼業が多かった組紐作りが独立して
専門の組紐師が増えてきた。さらに組紐の上で特筆すべきことは、「名護屋帯」とよ
ばれる組紐の帯が生まれたことである。これは、秀吉が朝鮮侵略の拠点とした肥
前(佐賀県)の名護屋で流行り始めたとされる帯で、八つ組みや丸唐組(16玉丸紐)
で組まれた5メートル位のものである。これを腰に5～6回まわし蝶結びにして
好みの位置に垂らしたという。朝鮮から連れてこられた工人が作り始めたもので、
当時「韓組帯」ともよばれていた。16世紀末から17世紀半ばまで大流行で、江戸時
代初期の風俗画にその様子が見受けられる。

　秀吉の豪放磊落な性格やその工芸の奨励が桃山文化を開花させる一助になった
と言えるだろう。

組紐の研究はなされたか？［江戸時代］

　この時代、天下太平になってからは、武士はまた外装にこるようになってきた。江戸には武士が50万人いたそうだから、その紐の消費量は莫大であったと考えられる。そこで、職人たちも京都などから移住して来て、江戸組紐にたずさわることになる。

　武士は、太刀、脇差の下緒（さげお）、柄巻、胴丸（どうまる）などの紐に組紐を用い、町人は、組帯、鏡台やふすま・たんすの飾り紐、種々の装飾紐として組紐を多用した。

　このように組紐は人々の生活に浸透した後、技巧を凝らしたものができ始め、高台や内記台の考案によってその傾向は一層強まった。ただし高台の出現によって足打台は衰退していったようである。

　江戸後期になると綾出しの紐が考案された。これは高台の一間組および二間組の二枚物で、表裏２色の糸を用いて柄を組み出すもので、真野家の平安重（たいらのやすしげ）が御嶽神社に復元奉納した両面亀甲組の両端にも綾出しで文字を組み出したものが見られる。

　この平安重のように自分で組紐を組む武士も現れはじめた。もっとも安重は代々甲冑研究家の家柄であり、その道に造詣が深かったわけだが、これとは別に組紐は、生活に追われた下級武士にとってかっこうの内職となっていった。

　江戸時代には、組紐に関する重要な資料や解説書が作られた。これまでそういうことがなされていなかったことを考えると、これは画期的なことであった。

　まず、元禄年間に加賀藩主前田綱紀が編さんした『百工比照』、これは工芸品の見本帖で、この中の紐の手鑑に101点の紐が集められている。次に1826年、下野黒羽藩主である大関増業の編さんになる『止戈枢要』の組訓備考３巻があり素晴しいものである。巻の一には、丸台、駿河打台（綾竹台）、高台の組み方や台の寸法、房の作り方、鎧の威などが記されている。巻の二は秘伝糸組で、手にループを掛けて足打台で組んだとされるものが、簡単な暗号を用いて記されている。巻の三は、さらに秘伝のもので、糸の撚（よ）り方、撚りの道具、両面亀甲の柄色割出しの図、ループ操作で簡単にきれいに組むための新案の台が載っている。

　この他、尾張藩士真野与市左衛門安代他編による『真野家伝糸組品々手附』、また現在組紐生産の最も多い伊賀に『柄糸組手本帳』と呼ばれる組紐の見本帖が残されている。（５図参照）これは、1790年ころ伊賀上野の城下中町（こしら）で、刀剣装具の拵（こしら）えを家業とした友生屋（とものや）忠兵衛が顧客のために作ったものである。しかし、これらの組紐が当時すべて伊賀地方で生産されたものかどうかはわからない。

組紐と新時代［明治以降］

　明治９年（1876年）の廃刀令により最大の用途であった刀関係の組紐の需要がなくなってしまった。職人たちは、これによりたちまち職を失うことになるが、東京の組紐師たちは、その技術を帯締めや羽織紐に生かすことにより何とか時代の波を乗り越えた。

　帯締めは、明治の後半になるまで現在のような組紐で作られたものではなく、丸ぐけ、平ぐけが一般的であった。丸ぐけの帯締めは、1817年、江戸亀戸天神の太鼓橋の渡り初めに深川の芸者衆が太鼓橋に似せた帯結びをしたときに使われたものが始まりと言われ、以来明治期に組紐の帯締めが組紐師によって製造されるまで続いた。日清戦争の頃（1894年）房の付いた組紐による帯締めが登場し、大変

に斬新だったため人気を呼んだ。これより少し前、男物の羽織紐に房のない「無双」（むそう）
と呼ばれる組紐が生まれていた。

　明治も後期になると一般庶民にも着物は入手しやすくなり、それに伴って帯締め
の需要が増し、漸次組紐の帯締めは一般化していった。

　明治の後半から昭和10年くらいまでは、明治政府の殖産興業策や数度の戦捷景気（せんしょう）
も手伝い経済は上向き、組紐は増々需要を高めていった。しかしその後、第二次大戦
による統制経済で繊維業界は全て材料不足となり、組紐は、儀礼章やラッパの紐と
いった軍需関係品に限られた。儀礼章は古代紫の糸で丸唐組や角八つ組に組まれ、飾
り結びにして国民服の胸を飾った。

　戦後、高度成長期を迎えると和装から洋装への転換が著しくなり、それに伴って
和装用品である組紐の需要は低下の道を辿り始めた。こうした状況に加えて組紐業
界にも機械化の波が押し寄せ、職人や組子たちの職場は一層狭くなった。

　昭和40年以降は、組紐を趣味として作り楽しむという方向が生じ、一時期ブーム
にさえなった。その後、組紐を和装用品に限ることなく広く役立てていこうとする
動きが芽生え、若い職人や研究者などの間で熱心な開発が行なわれ始めている。

主要参考文献

道明新兵衛『ひも』————————————————学生社　1963
井上光貞「日本の歴史・1」————————中央公論社　1965
山本茂貴『ひも物語』————————三重県組紐協同組合　1970
鷹司誓玉『唐組平緒』————————————————平凡社　1972
正倉院事務所『正倉院の組紐』————————————平凡社　1973
菅沼晃次郎『京くみひも』———————全京都組紐連合会　1978
山木　薫『くみひもの研究』————————総合秋学出版　1978
『組紐』————————————————————————泰流社　1978
土山弥太郎『組紐』————————————————私家版　1980
「組紐」(『なごみ』54)————————————————淡交社　1984
額田　巌『ひも』————————————法政大学出版局　1986
木下雅子「ループ操作組紐と日本の組紐」
(『染織α』4・5月号)————————————染織と生活社　1987
木下雅子「世界の組紐からみた文化の伝承と創造」
(「日本家政学会誌」Vol. 38　No.6　527〜530)—————————1987

組紐の技法

中内祥雄

組 台

　組紐は、大きく分類すると、丸組紐、角組紐、平組紐の三種に分けられる。組
台には、丸台、角台、綾竹台、高台の四種類が今日では一般的で、各台はそれぞ
れ特徴をもっているので、組紐の種類に応じて使い分けるとよい。(6－13図参照)

丸 台

　丸台には、上に組まれてゆく"組み上げ式"と下に組まれてゆく"組み下げ式"と
がある。組み上げでは、主に丸い紐が、組み下げでは、丸、角、平のいずれの紐
もできる。しかし、それぞれの特徴をより出そうとするなら綾竹台や高台を用い
る方が効果的である。

角 台

　ほとんどが丸台で組まれるものと同じであるが、玉数は丸台ほど多くすること
はできない。撚りを必要とする組みがほとんどで、組みの周囲を回るような動き
で組み上げてゆく。

綾竹台

　縦糸と横糸の交差によって組まれるため織りに近い組織となる。平紐ができる。
これは他のどんな台より効率良く、スピーディーに組める台で、それは玉が全て
手前に下げられるため扱いやすいこと、さらに上下左右、４つのＶ型刻みをもつ
板のそれぞれの刻みに掛けられた糸が、一手一回の動きで上段と下段の位置を入
れ替えるため、丸台の四手分に相当する綾をいっぺんにとることができるためで
ある。

高 台

　台の上に坐り、左右の糸の間に手をくぐらせて綾をとり、その綾の間から糸を
くぐらせて反対側に糸を運び、組み目を整えるために竹のヘラを打つ。百以上の
玉数が使えるので組み目を緻密にすることができ、文字など極めて具象的な柄模
様を表わすことが可能である。主に平紐が組まれる。

丸台による組み方

　ここでは、ひとつの例として最も適用範囲が広く、台そのものが簡単で使いや
すい丸台を用いて、丸四つ組の組み方を見てみよう。

道具・材料

　道具は、丸台のほかに糸束を巻く玉、錘り、箸、鋏、のり、櫛、針などが必要となる。玉は組み糸を巻きつけておくもので、中に錘りが入っていて100グラムの重さにしてある。4玉から36玉もあれば各種の組みが楽しめる。中錘りは、組み下げの引っ張る役をするもので、使用玉数全体の約半分くらいの重さにするのが目安。箸は組み糸を丸台に固定させるために必要となる。

　材料は絹糸で、通常、帯締め一本分が束になり袋に入って売られている。糸は、単糸を25本まとめてよりがかけられ、ひとまとめにされたものを1持と言い、それが24持ちまとめられて1束になっている。伸ばすと2.6メートルあり、帯締めの組み上り寸法、約1.5メートルとなる。

実技

　四つ組は4本の糸束で構成され、技術的には最も基本的なものである。一見簡単なように見えるが、組み目の不ぞろい、ゆるみといったものが、単純なだけに目立ちやすく、きれいな四つ組を仕上げるには熟練の手を要すと言われている。以下の説明は57−63頁の写真(Step 1〜12)を参照のこと。

1：1束(全玉分)の組み糸の端を約4センチくらい房のために残して、ゆるまないようにしっかりと結ぶ。

2：結ぶときの手の要領は、結び糸をたぐって手のひらを半分返し、輪をつくり、組糸の束をくぐらせてしっかりと締めつける。

3：丸台の穴から組み糸を巻きつけた箸を差し入れる。

4：台に糸をつけたところ。24持を4つに分け、それぞれの糸をきれいにさばき、互いにからまないようにする。

5：玉つけ。糸をピンと張ったまゝ組糸を巻いてゆき、台の近くまで来たら、右手に持った糸を捻じるようにして手のひらを半分ひっくり返して輪をつくり、玉にかぶせるようにしてかける。

6：錘りを入れた袋を組糸の端に付けているところ。ここまでで組むための準備が完了する。

7：姿勢を正しくして組み始める。右手で向こう側の糸を、左手で手前の糸を持つ。これは入れ替えが済んで置くところ。

8：手の動きを無駄にしないよう向こうに行った左手で右側の横糸をとり、左右の入れ替えをする。これは入れ替えをはじめた直後。

9：横糸の入れ替えが済んで置こうとするところ。

10：帯締めの約3分の1くらいが組み上ったところ。

11：房付けの準備。組み上った端の組目のきれいなところを結び、きちんと結ぶ。

12：結びがズレたり解けたりしないように紐の縦方向に糸でくくる。結び目の元に針を通してその準備をする。それから房を2つに分け、針で通した糸を房の中心で結ぶ。

近代の組紐と伊賀

中内祥雄

　今日、組紐のシェアの8割強は伊賀組紐（三重県）によって占められている。しかしその歴史は、占有率の高さに比べて新しく、1世紀にも満たない。江戸時代、江戸から伝わった技術は明治の初期に滅び、現在の技術はその後明治の後半になってから再び東京よりもたらされたものである。

　近代において、組紐の上に起こった最大の事件は廃刀令（明治9年）であった。これにより武具、馬具に関係をもつ職人や工人たちは深刻な打撃を蒙った。細工職人などは、美術工芸品の修理などに糊口をしのいだが、組紐師は潰滅状態となった。事実、伊賀では、この期に組紐の伝統は途絶えている。東京の組紐師たちは、羽織の紐や帯締めを、刀の下緒、鎧の威毛を組む技術を応用して組紐でつくり、辛くも変革する社会情勢に対応した。

　現在残されている明治期の記録によると、組紐は男物の羽織紐、帯締め、女物の羽織紐といった順で一般化していったと推測できるが、明治期の組紐で残存するのはほとんどが男物の羽織紐で、帯締めは明治の後半に至るまでは江戸時代からのしきたりで、丸ぐけ、平ぐけだったようである。

伊賀組紐の誕生

　伊賀上野に組紐の種が蒔かれたのは、明治35年、廣澤徳三郎という、当時23歳の青年によってである。彼は、14歳のとき知己のすすめで上京し鍋釜鋳物工場に奉公するが気がすすまず、結局、江戸組紐の技術をもつ小林栄之助と出会うことで高台の技術を修得することになる。何によらず職人の技というものは盗まぬ限り身につくものではなく、彼は住み込み奉公し、刻苦勉励、9年間の技術練磨のすえ郷里に工房を開くことになった。

　これが現在の伊賀組紐の生いたちであり、彼が特に高台の技術を学んだことは以後の伊賀組紐を特徴づけることになる。高台が、具象的な図柄や文字を組み出すことに適した台であることから、そうした製品が伊賀組紐の主力となってゆく。

明治後半から大正

　多少の時間的相異はともかく、東京でも伊賀でも帯締めに組紐が使われだしたのは、明治も中期を過ぎてからであった。明治政府の産業振興策が軌道に乗りは

じめるのが明治の中頃で、織物界では機械化が進み、化学染料が輸入され、それまで庶民には高嶺の花であった着物が身近なものになってゆく。銘仙の着物が一般の間に普及し始めるのが明治30年前後、こうした背景の中から組紐の帯締めが生れるが、最初は金具付きの、いわゆる"パッチン留め"といわれるもので、質の良い帯締めは大正時代を待たなくてはならなかった。

　伊賀の組紐は、廣澤徳三郎の開業以来順調な発展ぶりをみせるが、日露戦争（明治37年）のために注文がなくなり苦しい時期を迎える。しかしその後の戦捷景気によってほどなく活気を呈することになる。私の父中内源市（廣澤徳三郎の義兄）が開業したのもこんな時期だった。当時流行していた和服の復古調は好景気によって拍車をかけられ、それがまた和装全体の活性化につながった時代であった。着物の隆盛ぶりは昔日の比ではなく、たとえ文才があろうとも、女の着物を自由に書きこなす教養をもたなければ、作家にはなれないとさえ言われていたものだった。泉鏡花の『婦系図』（明治40年）は、絢爛たる女の着物をまるで仕立てるがごとく描いている。

　明治末期から大正にかけて、伊賀の組紐は、廣澤徳三郎の親戚、縁者を中心にその輪を広げてゆく。三重県立津高等女学校では、この時期、女性の教養として丸台組紐や「結び」を教科として行っており組紐の需要が一層高まっていったことを傍証している。当時、和装用以外では輸入ものの懐中時計の紐などに組紐は用いられたが、中心は何と言っても羽織紐と帯締めであり、需要の高まりが流行を生み、数々の種類をつくり出した。

　金具留めの帯締めは、現在でも京都の舞妓さんが着用する広幅のものと珊瑚や真珠などを金具に飾った細幅のものがあるが、一般には日露戦争以後ほとんど姿を消し、大正期には"組み"そのものの味を活かすものに趣向が移った。伊賀では、具象的な図柄や文字を得意とする高台が主力であったため、この組台で高麗組や地内記組の羽織紐、帯締めを相当量生産した。図柄は、古典的なものでは、矢絣、井筒、梅鉢などが時流に関係なくつくられ、一方四季折々の情緒をテーマとし、春は桜、夏は流れに舟、秋は菊や紅葉、冬は雪輪といった図柄が帯締めを新鮮なものにした。世相や流行を反映して、早慶戦のテーマでバットとボールといった図を、正月には毎年勅題にちなむ図柄を組み出すなどして人気を博した。

　高台以外でも市場の動向いかんでは丸台、角台、綾竹台にも取り組み注文に応じなければならなかったので、東京からそれぞれの組台の専門職人を呼び寄せたこともある。私が子どもの頃、東京から江戸っ子気質の丸台職人が住み込みで来ており、丸組を何寸組んだから、今は何時何分であるとピタリと言い当てたことをよく覚えている。

大正から昭和10年前後

　大正から第二次大戦の統制経済に至るまで着物も組紐も共に盛況を続けた。着物では、婦人ものに訪問着、散歩着が現われ、帯は丸帯に代わり着装が楽で軽快な狭幅の名古屋帯が考案された。組紐では、羽織紐、帯締め共に相当に幅が広くなり（羽織紐1センチ以上帯締め3センチ）、色調は当時の流行色であった紫、朱赤、黄緑や白と黒の対照を用いて様々な組み味を生かした製品が盛んにつくられた。(68－71頁参照)

　こうした盛況ぶりは、着物では電力による製織技術の近代化、人造絹糸の出現など原糸研究や応用の発展を促し、組紐では、機械化が進んでいなかった分だけ、

工房内で働く女工や家庭内職の婦女子の数を増やした。

　伊賀では、内職として藁仕事や機織りがあったが、組紐は、藁仕事よりはるかにきれいであるし、機織りより楽で収入がよかったこと、伊賀地方の風習として、娘を奉公や出稼ぎに出すことを嫌い、嫁入りするまで親の膝元においたこと、さらに伊賀には就職の場がほとんどなかったことなどにより、組紐は内職として大変な人気を集めた。伊賀の地に行けば、どこでも高台で紐を打つヘラ音が聞こえてきた。紐打ちの技術を持つ娘は嫁としても価値があり、嫁入りには高台を持ってゆくほどの状態であった。

　伊賀組紐の業態は、自ら製造販売するのではなく、京阪神地域の生産問屋に依存して賃加工をする下請専門業であったことが特徴で、この形態は、第二次大戦下の統制経済に入るまで続いた。今日と違い和服が主流であった当時では、問屋は冬には夏物を、夏には冬物を注文し、需要期になるまで持ち抱えて流通を調整するダムのような機能を果たしていた。問屋から染色された糸と注文書を受けとり、どこよりも早く安く仕上げることが要求され、その出来いかんで次の注文が決まった。

昭和10年〜戦後

　昭和に入ると次第に景気に翳りが見え始め、米の大暴落、失業者の増加など深刻な問題が生じだした。しかし組紐界は、なんとか無難な成長を示し、高麗、地内記、貝の口、笹波、大和打などさまざまな組みが行なわれた。昭和の初めまで13.5センチくらいだった女物の短い羽織紐（女短）は、体格の向上とファッション性から15センチほどになった。

　昭和10年を過ぎる頃から急激に軍国主義の色が濃くなり、昭和12年には、原料である正絹、人絹が割当配給となり、価格や規格が統制され、品質よりも規格が重要となっていった。昭和15年には、「奢侈品等製造販売制限規則」が発布され生糸の大部分はパラシュートや飛行服にまわされ、金銀糸はぜいたく品との指定を受けて使えず、業者の中には、せっかく組み上げた紐から苦労して金銀糸を抜き去る者もあった。戦時中は、国民服に着ける「儀礼章」のために古代紫の糸で丸唐組や角八つ組の紐を組むなどした。

　戦後、日本中が虚脱状態から回復しはじめた頃、組紐業者は軍需物資の払い下げであるパラシュートの紐や布地を材料に紐打ちを再開した。日本中が物資不足だったため、パラシュートの紐をそのまま1.5メートル位に切って染めれば売れる時代であった。いずれにしてもこの紐は正絹であり、下拵えのしやすい糸であったため素人でも比較的楽に扱うことができ、手っ取り早い現金収入の方法としても恰好であったため組紐を行う者が増えたわけである。戦前、問屋から糸を支給されて賃加工に甘んじていた業者は原材料の受給資格を得たことで、自分の糸で自家製品を作ることになった。

　この間の事情は、伊賀と東京では違っていた。東京では、関東大震災（大正12年）でかなりの痛手を蒙り、再び大戦で壊滅的打撃を受け土地は焦土と化し、四散した職人たちは戻るべき場を失い、転職を余儀なくされたようである。また業者が人手の確保をする場合でも東京より伊賀の方が有利で、戦後は伊賀が組紐の主たる生産地となってゆく。

　戦後も世の中が落着きだすと再び和装は人気をとり戻し、ブームとさえよべる時期をもたらした。帯締めは、太いものは野暮ったいということで細身になり、

模様は帯の柄とすっきりした対比をなすように無地に近くものになった。その代わり、組み自体に味を求める傾向が生じた。

　このような情況の中で、昭和29年、伊賀に初めて鉄製の機械が導入された。従来の手組み技術に近づけるべく機械組みに創意工夫を凝らすうちに需要も高まり、またそれが鉄製業者を増やしていった。

　日本経済が単なる復興を越えて高度成長の時期に入る昭和30年代以降、洋装が一般的になるに従い和服は晴れ着としての性格を強め、日常性を失ってゆく。組紐の需要はこれとともに低下し、一時的に昭和40年代半ば頃、組紐ブームが起こり、いわば趣味のひとつとして脚光を浴びるが、もともと生活に根差したものではなかっただけに組紐の低迷を救うまでには至らなかった。

　現在、伊賀組紐は、和装小物としてばかりでなく、広く生活全般に眼を向け、先人から伝えられたこの貴重な財産を生かすべく模索を続けている。

新しい分野に翔ける組紐

佐橋 慶

伊賀組紐の青年たちとの出会い

いまから6年前、私は伊賀組紐の若人たちと出会った。それまで、伊賀組紐の存在は知っていたが、まったく遠いものだった。

三十数年前、私は新聞記者時代に芭蕉を取材するためにこの地を訪れたことがある。しっとり落着いた城下町の風情に心が和んだことを憶えている。(16、17図参照)伊賀は芭蕉の生誕地であるばかりでなく、観世座を立てた観阿弥の故郷でもある。大阪にも京都にもまた名古屋にもほぼ等距離にある伊賀を徳川家康は、要害の地として特に念入りに築城するようにと伊賀領主藤堂高虎に命じたと伝えられている。

しかたのないことかも知れないが、以前に訪れたときの面影は大部薄れていた。格子戸の家並はとても風情があったが、それも姿を消しつつある。かつての紐打ちの盛況ぶりがなりをひそめたのも時の移ろいというべきか。お嫁に行くときは組台を持参し、農閑期には一刻をも惜しんで組紐を打ち家計を助けた。取材で町を歩いていると、どこの家からもカチカチ、トントンという高台のヘラ打ちの音が響いてきたものだった。

十数人の若者たち、二代、三代目の後継者である彼らから、何とかして衰退しはじめた組紐を再興させたいと相談を受けたとき、私はまず彼らの熱意にうたれた。彼らの情熱にほだされるままに何度か話し合いを重ね、ともかくも現状の改善と未来展望というスローガンのもとで団結し、事にあたる決意を固めた。これが伊賀組紐との出合いであり、出発であった。

1年目は現状の分析と方向付けをした。2年目は、和装以外の分野に進出しなければ活路は拓けないという認識から、他の分野、異業種の人々と意見を交換し、アドバイスを求めた。

伊賀組紐を取り巻く問題

それからしばらく仕事中断となった。再び伊賀組紐協同組合から声がかかったのは、今から2年前である。6年前の仕事とは異り、こんどは組合全体として現状打破をし、新しい分野に取り組みたいということで、以前の青年部の有志によ

113

る研究活動とは明らかに違ったものだった。

　この仕事を進めるにあたっては、古い体質に新しい息吹を吹き込むことが不可欠だが、それには現状の諸問題があまりに山積していて身動きがとれぬまでになっていると私には思えた。問題はおよそ次のようなものであった。

　衰退に向ってはいるものの、今のままでもまだ食べていかれるといった情況があること。飢餓感がないこと。これは先の情況に関連していることだが、結局このために思いきった進退の決意が出来ず、中途半端なこと。和装の付属品としての道を歩んできたため和装の動きに左右されてしまうこと。この関連で、和装物屋の流通に依存しているため新しい流通形態がとれないこと。組紐は、古典的、伝統的、高級品、美術品といったイメージが強く、そのため日常性、生活感といったところから遊離しやすいこと。

　以上のように数えあげれば際限のない障害が横たわっている。古い体質も改善し、人々の頭を180度転換しなければ一歩も進めないのが現状であるが、これはなにも組紐の世界にとどまらず、一般に伝統工芸といわれる世界には、程度の差こそあれ生じている問題ではないだろうか。

核になるものを持つこと

　空白の後、再び話がもちかけられたとき、私は従来の仕事の進め方、やり方では以前と同じ中途半端な仕事になると思った。そこで伊賀組紐に携わる人々がある目標に向けて情熱とロマンを燃やして一丸となってゆけるものはないか、これを作ることから仕事をはじめようとした。

　情熱をぶつける目標—核には何が最も適しているか、私は考えあぐねた結果それは本だと思った。本ができ、方向が打ち出されたら作品がついて来る、流通も、売り方も、そして人々も—。

　すでに組紐に関する本は何冊か出ている。特に解説書、実用書が多いが、同じ類の本を出しても仕方ない。それならば、従来の組紐という概念にとらわれず、組紐の新しい分野をめざし、誰にでも親しめ、自然に組紐が欲しくなってしまうような本にしたい、それも日本人だけでなく、海外の人々の気持をもうばってしまうような本をと考えた。そんな矢先、講談社インターナショナルの編集の人々に巡り合い、この本の話はとんとん拍子に進んでいった。ラッキーだった。

色の革命が始まった

　かつて組合の主宰する組紐展に出かけ、陳列ケースの中をのぞいたとき、私の気持は決った。まず第一に着手しなければならないことは色の革命において他にない。世の中の色が動き、着ものの色も変化をみせているのに組紐だけが立ち止まっている。これは何とかしなければいけない。色は伊賀組紐の突破口だと思った。

　ではどうすればよいか。早速編集会議がもたれ、メリハリのある色使いのコシノジュンコさんにお願いすることになった。イタリア、フランスそして近年の中国と国際的に活やくしている彼女の理解と、それにもまして情熱はすばらしかった。

　こうして、従来の組紐の色見本とは全く異なるJKカラーで染められることになった。今までの色見本に慣れていた眼には、これはカルチュラル・ショックとも言うべきもので、新鮮な驚きとともに戸惑いもかくせなかったようである。と

もかく新しい息吹が吹き込まれるようになったわけだが、ＪＫカラーをどのようにしたら忠実に再現できるか組合の人々の研究が始まった。色の点で、これとは別に工夫されなければならないことは、褪色や変色、また汚れなどに強い染色法や素材を開発していかねばならないということで、この点でも組合の若い人々の努力が重ねられた。

組紐を新たな素材で

色彩に限らず、素材の開拓も大きな課題である。コシノさんから提案された新素材にはさまざまのものがあったが、中でもひとつの試みとして、デザインとともに金属の糸が示され、一同を大変驚かせたことがあった。従来の組台でも鉄製の機械でも思うようにいかず、彼らは固い金属糸を相手に指先を傷だらけ、血だらけにした。

今では新しい素材としていろいろなものが実験されている。金属糸でも鋼鉄線で組まれたベルトはスチールベルトとしてタイヤに使われているし、銀線は、そのままで、あるいはメッキされてアクセサリーなどに用いられる。化学繊維では、原料の段階で着色されたテトロンやナイロンが実験的にではあるが組紐の素材として用いられだした。ペルーやボリビアの組紐（72頁参照）の素材である獣毛を日本の組紐に生かす方向も考えられている。

新しい分野でやってみると

組紐は、帯締め、羽織紐の世界から離れて、さまざまの分野で使われ、私たちの生活を豊かにそして楽しくしてくれることと思う。たとえば、ファッション関係では、ネクタイやベルトにあるいはパッチワーク風の使い方をしたり、ベストなどにはそのまま組紐が生かせるだろう。

小物関係では、バッグ、ショルダー類の紐、ウエストバッグのベルト、カメラや時計の紐、帽子の飾り、ペンダントやネックレスなどアクセサリーの紐など応用範囲が広い。

インテリア関係では、タピストリー、間仕切り、のれん、すだれとして、ロールアップブラインドやカーテンの留め紐としてしゃれた結びを取り入れて用いるのもよく、結びはタンスの引き手などにも応用できる。この他椅子の背もたれ、クッションの縁どり、テーブルクロス、テーブルセンター、ランチョンマット、コースターと用途は大変に広いと思う。(20－30図参照)

私自身は、ネクタイ、ベルト、ショルダーの紐、草履などに組紐を用いることがある。ネクタイ、ベルトは締めた感じが快く、長時間使用していても型くずれがしにくい。ショルダーバッグの紐は、肩からすべり落ちにくいので使い勝手がよく、しかも肌に触れたときには絹のしなやかさが感じよい。草履の履き心地は、皮製、布製とはひと味ちがい、歩くたびにきゅっきゅっときしみ、それが気持を和ませてくれる。

海外に出かけた折など持参した組紐でカーテンを飾ったり、小さく結んでナイフやフォーク置きにしたり、そのときどきで趣向をこらし組紐の味わいを楽しんでもらうようにしている。評判がいいのは、組紐が海外のファッションやインテリアにもよく似合い調和するからだろう。

このように利用者が、各人の好みや目的に合わせて自由に組紐を楽しめるようになるには、ネクタイやアクセサリーをはじめ組紐の製品が豊富にそろうことと、

さらにいろいろなものに利用できるように“素材”としての組紐が充実することが必要になってくると思う。材質を変え、色や柄に変化をもたせ、玉数や組み方の違ったものをいろいろ用意する。さらに好きな長さや幅で買えるようにすれば利用度も使う楽しみも倍加するだろう。

新しい時代に先取りを

　これからの時代は、いよいよ私たちの生活は多様化し、各人がそれぞれの生活パターンに合わせてものごとを取捨選択してゆくだろう。私は、「伝承塾」を主宰しているが、日本の伝統工芸を墨守するのではなく、伝統の中に横たわる宝物を、多様化する私たちの生活に合わせて工夫し、より良いものへと磨き上げ、次の世代にバトンタッチしてゆくことが大切なことだと思っている。

　組紐も、単に先人の技をなぞるのではなく、明日を先取りする進取の気をもって創意工夫を重ねてゆかなければならないと思う。それこそが、「古人の跡を求めず、古人の求めたところを求める」という伊賀上野が生んだ俳聖芭蕉の言葉に通じるものと思っている。

カラー図版解説
(数字はページ数を表わす)

1　高台で途中まで組まれた高麗組の紐
ここに使われている藍、緑、紫、白、赤、黄の6色は正倉院の基調色といわれる古代色の代表。このうち藍(古い色彩名で縹色)は特に代表的な色で、"藍"といえば「染料」そのものを意味したときもあった。従って、古く中国より渡来した染料「くれない」(紅)は、「呉(中国)の藍(染料)」という意味だった。

当時の染色法で最も素朴なものは、衣に植物などをこすりつける草木染で、万葉集にはそのことを歌ったものが散見される。

　　住吉の　浅沢小野の　かきつばた
　　衣に擢り付け　着む日　知らずも　　　　(1361)

かきつばたの花は青味がかった紫色の染料、そしてここでは、「年頃の娘」の意味でもある。衣に擢り付け……にも「女性を妻として迎える」という別の意味が重ねられ

こすりつけて染色するだけでなく、既に媒染を用いた染色法も知られていた。

　　紫は　灰さすものぞ　海石榴市の
　　八十の衢に逢へる子や誰れ　　　　(3101)

紫染めに用いる紫草は、当時大変貴重な草、これは、アルミ分を含んだ椿の灰を媒染とすることでよく発色した。

2-3　糸巻きに巻かれた糸
色は現在用いられているもの。これらの糸は、房付け用にとってある。

4　高台に掛けられた玉
ひとつ100グラムが基準。通常、帯締めで74玉ぐらいが最多玉数となる。

閑崎ひで女氏の作品
閑崎ひで女氏は地唄舞、閑崎流の家元。地唄舞とは京都を中心に伝えられた女の舞い。生田流の地唄筝曲に舞いをつけたもので、本来座敷で道具など用いずに一人で舞うもの。地唄舞には恋の舞いが多く、氏は、現代に生きる女の心を舞ってみたいと言う。

海外での活やくもめざましく、アヴィニオン(フランス)の芸術祭をはじめ近年のミラノ・スカラ座の公演に至る様々な舞台で高い評価を得ている。

組紐で一番心を配った点は、舞い同様、古来からの美しい形を大切にしながら、そこに新しいものを盛ることだと言う。

10　「鑑」
正月の飾りで、お餅に代えてお米を供えた。七色の組紐を結んで添えて、正月の厳かな中に華やかさを演出。

11　「七夕」
祈りをこめて組紐を結ぶ。結びの形と色を楽しむ。

本来「結び」には、実用的な目的のほかに精神世界の出来事を表現するという大きな役割があった。時代を遡れば遡るほどこの役割は動かしがたく、深く人の心に根を張っていた。

それが平安時代になって有職故実の中に法則化され、服飾をはじめ室内装飾などいろいろなところで結びは多用され、宮廷の女性たちは、和歌や管弦とならぶ教養として「花結び」を学ぶこととなった。

時代が移り武士が登場すると、結びは鎧兜など武具に用いられる一方、文化面では、茶道や香道の発達が新たな結びを生み出すことになる。たとえば、封印することを目的とした仕覆(茶入れを保護する袋)の結びは、中身のすり替えや毒物の投入を防ぐために複雑を極め、結び方は秘中の秘とされた。(32図参照)

武家文化の装飾結びの集大成は『包結の記』(1764)となうて現れ、水引きから手箱、軸物、長刀鞘袋など50種におよぶ結びの使用法が図説されている。(33図参照)

このように様々に発達し、形式化した「結び」ではあるが、その根本には実用を越えて結びに精神性や神秘性をみる人々の心が宿っている。(34図参照)

11　「祝膳」
名取り式の祝いの膳。菜、鳥、ソウ麺を具とした汁に昆布、スルメ、梅干を添える。菜・鳥でナトリ、昆布は喜コブ、スルメは噛むほどに味が出る。梅干は皺のよるまでの意。梅の赤は"艶"に通じる。

12　「舞」
地唄舞を土台に、今日の音楽、組紐という小道具を用いた新しい演出で女の舞いを試みた。

14-36　コシノジュンコ氏の作品
現在最も活やくしているファッションデザイナーの一人。コスチュームのデザインをはじめ、舞台・映画衣裳、ユニフォームのデザイン、あるいは日用品やインテリアデザインなどにも意欲的に取り組み、トータルコーディネーターとして幅広い活動をしている。

海外での活やくもめざましく、パリ、ミラノ、北京、台北などに出店し好評を博している。

組紐についてコシノ氏は、「宇宙は全て円で出来ている。人の手でからめて円く形にしていくのも組紐。その円という仕組みからイメージしたものを作ってみた」と語っている。

14-15　「スパイラル」

16-17　白と黒のカーテンリング

多田美波氏は現代日本を代表する彫刻家の一人。ステンレス、アクリル、ガラスなどの素材を用いた立体造形で新分野を拓いた。

　作品には彫刻ばかりでなく建築の空間造形・照明関係のデザインも多くいずれも大変高い評価を得ている。

　組紐と氏とのつき合いは長く、その魅力に出合って以来組紐を蒐集し、またいつかは作品に取り入れたいと思ってきたと言う。とりわけガラスの作品には金属より組紐の方が馴染みがよく、千変万化するガラス作品の光彩に組紐の複雑な綾がよく調和し、お互の良さを発揮してゆく。

伝統の組紐

65　金銅装唐組垂飾(法隆寺献納宝物)
重文　平組紐　幅 5.5cm　飛鳥時代
東京国立博物館保管
推古天皇の几帳の垂飾として使われていたといわれる。茜を基調とした色彩は今なお鮮やかで、いかにも大陸からの渡来を感じさせる色調である。渡来品でなければ、大陸より帰化した職人の労作であろう。
　二菱の唐組(菱形模様を出した平組紐。V字模様を交互に反転して出す)で菱の形が縦方向に長いので唐組台を使用していると思える。
　後年、束帯で用いられる平緒は、この唐組が発展したもの。

65　紺紙金字一切経帙の組紐
重文　平組紐　幅2cm　平安時代
神護寺旧蔵(京都)
後白河法皇が高雄の神護寺に奉納した一切経を十巻ごとに巻き綴じる帙(竹簀を飾り編みしたもの)とY字に取り付けられた平組みの緒。これは組の方がゆるいので指だけの操作で組まれたものと考えられる。

66　錦包懸守の紐
国宝　断面長方形の角組紐　幅1cm　厚さ0.5cm　平安時代
四天王寺蔵(大阪)
懸守は女性が詣でなどの旅中、胸前に懸けた守り。懸守は檜材で形成、表面は各種の錦で包んだ。組紐は、4畝×6畝の角組。これはループ操作で組まれたと考えられる。
通常の角組では、縁にみる糸は内部を通過して反対側の面に出て模様を形成することになるがこの紐は縁の糸が常に縁にしか出ない特別の組み方をしている。

66　平緒
(上)「紫絲尾長鳥文繍唐組続平緒」
平組紐　長さ2m64cm　房の長さ26cm×2　幅8.4cm
(中)「薄櫨綾和歌浦古歌葦手文繍唐組続平緒」平組紐

長さ2m57cm　房の長さ23cm×2　幅8cm
(下)「縹地牡丹連鵲文繍唐組続平緒」
平組紐　長さ2m9cm　房の長さ23cm×2　幅8cm
江戸時代(3点とも)
大道 久氏蔵(撮影/小林庸浩)
平安時代以後、衣冠束帯は貴族の正装となり、束帯には平緒を用いることが有職故実に定められていた。唐組の平緒は高位(五位以上)の貴族のみに許されていたため、身分、権威を象徴するものとなった。平緒の繊細な図柄や色使い、組みの細やかさは、組紐工芸の中でも格調が高い。
　ここにみる平緒は、菱形が精密であり、暈繝(色のぼかし)が配されていることなど唐組がすっかり日本化したことを示している。

67　装束類両面亀甲の紐
国宝　断面長方形の角組紐　幅1.4cm　厚さ0.5cm　平安時代
熊野速玉大社蔵(和歌山県)　(撮影/小林庸浩)
同社に伝わる六条の紐の一つ。用途は不明。4畝×8畝の角組でループ操作法によったと推定できる。72ループ(玉数にすれば、144玉)を要し、片手に9ループずつ、両手で18ループを掛けた人間が4人でループを交換して作ったと考えられる。

67　赤糸威鎧
国宝　鎌倉時代　櫛引八幡宮蔵(青森県)
豪華な装飾金物は、精緻を極めており鎌倉末期の金工芸術の精華といえるもの。本体の作りも精巧。社伝では長慶天皇(1343~94)の御料という。
　威毛は一枚ものの平組紐、忍緒は組紐ではなく丸ぐけ、繰締緒は片面亀甲模様の厚みのある平緒。耳糸も片面亀甲文平紐。
　この鎧は、戦争直前に盗難に遭い、間もなく発見され、戦後補修された。なお金属部分は鎌倉時代当時のまま。

68-69 **伊賀の帯締め**
昭和初期から戦後ぐらいまでに現われた二枚ものの平組
帯締め。二枚ものとは平組の組紐が二枚重ねられた状態
になっている帯締めで、表と裏が別々の層であるため、
表裏の糸を入れ替えて組むことにより具象的で細かい図
柄などが出せる。伊賀を代表する組紐で、高台によって
組まれる。

70-71 **伊賀の羽織り紐**
　大正から昭和初期にかけての平組の羽織紐。一枚もの、
二枚もの、幅の広いもの狭いものなどいろいろ。木箱内
の紐と外に出ている柄ものは女もの。現在は、洋装感覚
から女ものは羽織の色に合わせて同系の色とする傾向に
あるが、当時は派手な配色、柄ものが多かった。

72 **ペルーの投石器**
多田牧子氏蔵
クレードル(亀裂のはいった幅広の部分)に石を乗せ、そ
こから紐を二つ折りにし、紐の両端をもって振り回し、

片端をはなして石を飛ばす。戦闘や狩猟の際に使われた。
　投石器は手だけを道具として組まれる。片手を丸台が
わりにし、何本かの獣毛糸(羊、アルパカなどの)を持ち、
糸の位置を交換して組んでゆく。獣毛糸は絹糸と違いす
べりにくいので錘りの必要はなく、毎段締めながら組み
進む。ただしクレードルは織物になっている。
　色彩がボリビアのものに比べて落着いているのは、獣
毛の色をそのまま生かしているから。色とりどりに染め
られた球飾りのついた紐は祭りのとき踊りに使われる。

72 **ボリビアの投石器**
多田牧子氏蔵
作り方はペルーのものと同じ。こちらのクレードルの菱
柄は手だけで組まれている。
　素材もペルーの場合と同じで、昆虫や植物などで鮮や
かに染色されている。
　現在でも、これらの紐は組まれ、使われている。

白黒図版解説
(数学は図版ナンバーを表わす)

1 埴輪　礼装の男子像
重文　高さ124.2cm　6世紀頃(古墳時代)
相川考古館蔵(群馬県)
二重に紐かがりした大きな美豆良を肩に垂らし、衣は1
ヶ所紐で結び、衣褌は足結いしてひだを作っている。高
位の人物とみられる。

2 幡縁飾組紐(法隆寺献納宝物)
重文　平組紐　長さ65cm　幅3.5cm　飛鳥時代
東京国立博物館保管
茜と紫色を交互に配し矢羽根模様を組み出した笹浪組と
呼ばれる組紐。幡の縁飾とは、仏教で用いられる旗、幡
の緑を美しく飾る紐。色の使い方は大陸的。

3 雑帯(正倉院宝物)
正倉院には後世の種々の組紐の基礎的要素を備えている
各種の組紐がある。文様は斜線構成の幾何学的なものに
なり、配色はきわめて豊かで、その色彩感覚は大陸的。
(上)雑帯
平組紐　長さ132.2cm　幅4.7cm前後　奈良時代
正倉院蔵(奈良県)
　これは二間組の平帯で、礼服の条帯と考えられている。
(下)雑帯
平組紐　長さ214.4cm　幅6cm前後　奈良時代
正倉院蔵(奈良県)
これは一間組の平帯で、現在「安田組」と呼ばれている手
法にあたる。

4 『七十一番職人歌合』より「組師」
江戸時代の模本　東京国立博物館蔵
足打台で組紐を組んでいる。指にかけたループを交換し
て組み進むごとに足でヘラを操作してヘラ打ちをし、組
み目を締める。熟練することによって迅速に、また複雑
なものが組める。

5 『柄糸組手本帳』
江戸末期、伊賀上野で刀剣装具を商っていた友生屋忠兵
衛が客のために用意した柄糸の見本帳。

6 丸台

7 丸台で組まれた平組の例

8 角台

9 角台で組まれた平組の例

10 陵竹台

11 陵竹台で組まれた平組の例

12 高台

13 高台で組まれた平組の例

14 高台での作業風景
右手で竹のヘラを打ちこみ、左手で陵をとっている。

15 『六十余州名所図会』(安藤広重画)より「伊賀上野」
19世紀半ごろの様子。坂道を登ったところに伊賀上野城
が望まれる。

新しい組紐の世界
発 行   1988年2月29日
編 者   佐橋 慶
訳 者   モニカ・ベーテ
発行者   服部敏幸
発行所   講談社インターナショナル株式会社
          東京都文京区音羽1-2-2 〒112
          電話 東京(03)944-6491(代表)
          振替 東京3-26173
印 刷   大日本印刷株式会社
製 本   株式会社黒岩大光堂
©講談社インターナショナル株式会社 1988
Printed in Japan

協力
伊賀くみひもセンター
三重県組紐協同組合
〒518 三重県上野市四十九町1929-10
電話 0595(23)8038

定価2,800円
in Japan